How To Get An Athletic Scholarship

A Student-Athlete's Guide
to Collegiate Athletics

by DISCARDED

Whitney Minnis

ASI Publishing, Washington, DC DISCARDED

How To Get An Athletic Scholarship:
A Student-Athlete's Guide To Collegiate Athletics

© Copyright 1995 by Whitney Minnis

Published by ASI Publishing
512 15th St., S.E., Suite 100
Washington, DC 20003
202-547-0355
ASI Publishing is a Division of Alphanumeric Systems, Inc.

Cover art work courtesy of Corel, Inc., Ontario, Canada.

Library of Congress Catalog Card Number: 95-75835

Publishers' Cataloging in Publication
(Prepared by Quality Books Inc.)

Minnis, Whitney.
　　How to get an athletic scholarship :a student-athlete's guide to collegiate athletics / by Whitney Minnis.
　　　　p. cm.
Includes bibliographical references and index.
ISBN 0-9645153-0-X

1. Sports--Scholarships, fellowships, etc.--United States. 2. College sports--United States. I. Title.

GV583.M56 1995　　　　　　　796'.079'73
　　　　　　　　　　　　　　QBI95-20299

How To Get An Athletic Scholarship

Table of Contents

To Dad, who devoted countless energy, resources and time to train, support, and encourage me.

To Mom, who always believed in me.

To my coaches, and teachers who gave more than what was required.

Preface

"Don't let athletics use you. You use athletics," a high school coach once told me. That advice paid off well for me. My athletic scholarship, in soccer, did more for me than provide me with an education—it gave me a jump on life. I graduated from college debt free, an established credit rating in hand, and a job waiting for me. And best of all, my education didn't cost my parents a dime!

My athletic achievements were not so great, I wasn't an All-American, I wasn't All-State, or even a first team All-County selection. Yet, by the end of my senior year in high school I had amassed dozens of scholarship offers in three sports! I was able to get those offers by following many of the techniques and principles that I describe in the pages that follow.

I hope the information in this guide will be an inspiration for student-athletes, and parents as well. Opportunities for athletic scholarships are very realistic for athletes who are not All-Americans, or All-State selections—I'm proof of that! Athletic scholarships will be granted only to athletes who have the heart and desire to persevere through adversity.

Athletics can create many opportunities and rewards for those who are prepared to receive them. I encourage you to be selfish and take full advantage of those opportunities and rewards, because they do not last long.

I'm taking my coach's advice one step further in writing this book and, in so doing, hopefully, inspiring others to fulfill their goals. I'm not the preaching type, but, I hope that as you pursue your athletic (and other) goals, you keep an aspect of spirituality in mind. I honestly believe that if one works hard enough, prays (or meditates) hard enough, and maintains a true belief in his or her abilities, the opportunities will come. The following quote is from biblical scripture in the book of Mark, 11:23-24. It has been a never ending source of inspiration for me:

"For verily I say unto you, That whosoever shall say unto this mountain, Be thou removed, and be thou cast into the sea; and shall not doubt in his heart, but shall believe that those things which he saith shall come to pass; he shall have whatsoever he saith. Therefore I say unto you, What things soever ye desire, when ye pray, believe that ye receive *them*, and ye shall have *them*."

Introduction

    This guide is written to provide basic information of the availability of athletic scholarships. Whether a student-athlete, coach, or parent, we hope that the information in this guide leads you to fulfilling your goals. We believe the student-athlete who applies the information and techniques described in this guide, will greatly enhance his or her chances to receive an athletic grant-in-aid (athletic scholarship).

    Although this guide includes specific techniques for generating interest and receiving offers, it is in no way exhaustive. The "Recommended Reading" section at the end of the book includes further resources to assist you in your decision making.

    The title reflects only part of our goal for the student-athlete. Our purpose, above all, is to provide information to the student athlete that will not only enable him to get an athletic scholarship, but keep one as well. In most cases, throughout the guide, we will not refer to "minimum" standards, i.e. eligibility standards. The most current information can be made readily available by contacting your prospective college association, or through your high school athletic director. The student-athlete benefits greater by "exceeding" the minimum standards in each endeavor he chooses—academics and athletics as well. Student-athletes, who pursue minimum standards, do not get athletic scholarships!

In our effort to cover the subject of athletic scholarships as clearly as possible, we are limiting the subject to the following:

•   The information can be applied to the three major intercollegiate governing bodies: NCAA (National Collegiate Athletic Association) , NAIA (National Association of Intercollegiate Athletics), and the NJCAA, (National Junior College Athletic Association). The NJCAA is an organization whose member schools are two-year colleges (also known as community colleges or junior colleges).

• The NCAA's Division III is not a consideration of this guide since an athletic scholarship is not offered in this division.

• Ivy League schools are not a consideration since they too do not offer athletic scholarships.

The most beneficial scholarship award is the full athletic scholarship. It is the one to which we hope you will aspire. However, partial scholarships, a full scholarship divided among two or more athletes, are not uncommon. In many instances, these scholarship awards suit the needs of athletes very well. The full athletic scholarship is an athletic scholarship (grant-in-aid) given to a qualified student-athlete to cover the full costs of tuition, room, board, and books at a college or university. For our purposes, a collegiate student-athlete is both 1) an amateur athlete eligible to compete in intercollegiate athletics and, 2) a degree candidate working towards an undergraduate or post-graduate degree.

Although we would like to think that the techniques and tips (in the chapters that follow) work equally well in all sports, in practice they do not. We do believe any student-athlete will get some benefit from this guide, but our primary focus centers around athletes involved in the following sports: football, basketball, baseball, hockey, soccer, gymnastics, tennis, wrestling, lacrosse, track & field, volleyball, swimming, and golf. Female and male athletes can benefit equally from the information contained in this guide. The information in the guide is primarily directed to boys and girls age nine to eighteen.

College Scholarship Trends

Scholarships are available for student-athletes who qualify themselves to receive them. Qualification is determined by displays of skills and abilities in and out of the classroom. As the following figures indicate, student-athletes cycle through the collegiate scene fairly regularly, annually creating opportunities for new prospects. There are plenty of athletic scholarships available and here are just a few reasons why:

•   The drop-out rate for young athletes is tremendously high. A study revealed that as many as 80 percent of all youth who compete in organized sports between the ages of 12 and 17, drop-out (Hopper, 1988).

•   Every year, in the NCAA's division I & II, about 175,000 men and women are on scholarship. In the NAIA there are over 65,000 men and women on scholarship. These scholarships are issued or renewed annually (not every four years).

•   There are over 500 member NJCAA institutions offering one and two-year athletic scholarships.

•   In total, there are over 2,000 colleges and universities (including two-year and four-year schools), throughout the country, offering athletic scholarships.

•   An NCAA study (The NCAA News, July, 1991) reported the following (this study excludes member NAIA and NJCAA institutions):

• Twenty-five percent of entering freshmen student-athletes leave school within the first two years (approx. 44,000).

• Less than one in two student-athletes (approx. 46%) graduate within five years.

• Over half the student-athletes entering college today will *leave* school within five years without a degree.

• Of all the student-athletes that enter collegiate athletics, less than five percent of the student-athletes continue on to graduate after the fifth year—many without the benefit of a grant-in-aid (scholarship).

• As you can see there are many athletic scholarship opportunities available to *qualified* student-athletes, on a regular basis. Qualified student-athletes being those student-athletes who can meet the academic and athletic demands of the college level.

College Education Costs

You may have bought this guide because you realize what a college education costs today. Hopefully, with this reference you will be able to utilize your God given talents to fulfill your collegiate goals.

Public Education Costs

The cost of a college education is outpacing inflation. In fact, on average, household incomes have not been able to keep pace with the double digit increases of college costs. For example, in 1993 the average annual cost of a public university was $5,772. The expected annual cost in the year 2003 is $14,972 (Chany, 1992).

Private Education Costs

If you're not suffering from sticker shock yet, the average annual cost of a private college in 1993 was $14,250. The expected annual cost in the year 2003 is $28,032 (Chany, 1992).

To The Year 2000 And Beyond

Obviously, there is no way to tell what future costs will be. However, by receiving an athletic scholarship, just as with other scholarships created by an institution, the full value of the award will always meet an institution's direct costs for tuition, room, board, and books. Once an athletic scholarship is granted to a student-athlete, although technically an annual award, it can not be taken away as a result of injury, or because of under-performance. The award must be given, if a student-athlete maintains athletic and academic eligibility (refer to the appropriate governing body's manual for more specifics). Even if an institution cuts its athletic program, its scholarship athletes will most likely retain their awards through graduation.

The financial background from which a student-athlete comes is immaterial in the awarding of a scholarship. Athletic scholarships are given to student athletes because they can perform on the field and in the classroom. Financial hardship or prosperity is not a consideration for a coach who wants to win games.

What Does This Book Contain?

Earning an athletic scholarship is a process. Each chapter attempts to identify key aspects towards the fulfillment of the goal of receiving an athletic scholarship.

Chapter 1 addresses issues affecting youth development. How do I develop the athletic talent in my youth? How do I nurture the talent that now exists? The answers to these questions and more are answered to, hopefully, bring to a close any doubts regarding natural versus nurtured abilities.

Chapter 2 focuses on the student-athlete. In it, we attempt to disect the athlete's motivation and put in to focus the energy required to achieve multiple offers. The self-inventory is the beginning. It is in this chapter that we address the personal needs and wants of the student-athlete.

Chapter 3 looks at the college game. What should the student-athlete know if he expects to receive a scholarship at a two or four year institution? We discuss eligibility, the *seven key elements* recruiters evaluate before they consider making an offer and more.

Chapter 4 focuses on creating the success plan. Our objective is to discuss options which put the student-athlete on the best possible path to an athletic scholarship.

Chapter 5 highlights resources, sites, and events available to athletes. We briefly discuss options for making contact, soliciting and receiveing offers for an athletic scholarship.

In *Chapter 6* we discuss the issues of diet and injury prevention.

Chapter 7 mentions pointers that can be used before, during and after competition. You will find tips on training and academics that can be used at the high school and college level.

In the *Appendicies and Other Back Matter* section you will find training routines, bibliography, index, and a recommended reading section.

Disclaimer

This publication is designed to provide accurate and authoritative information with regard to the subject matter covered. It is sold with the understanding that the author and publisher are not engaged in rendering legal, medical, or other professional advice.

Every attempt has been made to make this book as accurate as possible. There may be mistakes of content or typography, however, and the author and publisher make no guarantees, warranties, or representations of any kind. This book is designed as a general guide to the subject. The reader is urged to investigate and verify information and its applicability under any particular situation or circumstances.

The author and publisher shall have no liability or responsibility to anyone with respect to contacts, negotiations, or agreements that may result from information in this book, or for any loss or damage caused or alleged to have been caused directly or indirectly by such information. If expert professional assistance is required, the services of a competent professional person should be sought.

Chapter One

Youth Development

Positive and active parental involvement is a strong factor in the success of a student-athlete. There are many facets of parental involvement. The key to being involved in the development of youth is to provide stability. The average youth will reach their objectives if they have a dependable environment of support.

As a youth coach, I understand how difficult it is to manage kids, (along with all the other responsibilities of life). The results of providing a stable support mechanism are realized in the youths consistent performance. If a youth is inconsistent in his performance then you will want to take a look at the major influences that effect performance: Rest, Diet & Health, Practice Sessions (their duration and frequency), Extracurricular Activities, and Social Life. The discussions that follow explain roles that you can take as parents that can positively influence children.

The Parent Coach

It is quite possible that some time during your youths development you may be put in a position to coach your youth or his team. I believe the endless hours my father spent with me in our personal training sessions both enhanced our relationship and made it possible for me to ascend through the college level. To get to the college level, you have to do more than what is required at team practice sessions. However, there are three different types of Parent Coaches.

The Passive Approach

The passive coach is the individual who has very little knowledge or interest in the sport itself. His interest is to spend "quality" time with his child in an effort to develop a bond. During practice sessions the youth will control and direct the sessions, but will be frustrated by the lack of knowledge or ability of the parent to make a constructive contribution. It is understandable that not all caring and supportive parents have athletic talent. But, sometimes youths see ineptness as weakness and therefore would rather spend their time playing and practicing with youths their own age. To overcome this problem, parents can first, read up on the sport. Attend coaching clinics, go to professional events with the youth, and attend the youth's practice sessions whenever possible. The goal is to be conversant in both the rules and strategy of the sport. Never underestimate the respect and admiration, <u>knowledge</u> will command from a youth! If it is your desire to see that your youth is the best that he can be, send him to specialized camps or hire personal trainers to develop the youth.

The Drill Sergeant

The drill sergeant is the opposite of the passive coach. The drill sergeant is the former "star" athlete (or want-to-be) who knows everything there is to know about the sport. He will attempt to influence the coach at practice and during games. Individualized training sessions are mandatory if his son or daughter is going to play a sport. Winning is the only thing, and one hundred percent effort at all times is expected. If the child loses or makes a bad play he will know that his mother or father will have something to say about it.

It is unfortunate but this situation is all to common in youth sports. The youth is put in a position where there are only two possible outcomes, success or failure. The youth gains acceptance by winning or chooses to leave sports all together because of the pressure to be the best. I believe the drill sergeant is the major contributor to the majority of youth burn-out cases in sports today. Unfortunately, many drill sergeants do not see themselves as the problem. They believe if it were not for their aggressive nature, they would not be successful. For some, a video tape of their behavior during a practice session or game may be sobering.

The Moderate Approach

The moderate coach approaches his contribution with an open mind. The parent is always supportive of the youth and his goals. The lines of communication are open and the parent has both an understanding of the rules and strategy of the sport. All attempts to play against the best competition and to receive the best coaching are made. The emphasis to "win" is never placed upon a child. Rather, the child is given performance goals (Spink, 1988) to which, success can be measured. For example, rather than give the golfer the objective of making a birdie on every hole or reaching a certain course score, keeping the ball in safe play may be an objective. As for the short game, making sure that each putt passes the hole as opposed to playing short may be another goal. In team sports (i.e. hockey, lacrosse, soccer or football) playing good defense is always in the athletes control. I don't believe that one can have a bad game defensively, if he hustles on every play and takes care of his responsibility first.

Sport Selection

As with the selection of an occupation, the selection of a sport must be made with careful consideration and an understanding of one's abilities and interests. To compare athletics, especially an athletic college career, with the selection of an occupation is not a far stretch when you consider that many athletes will spend about 10-15 years training and honing their athletic skills. It is advisable that as the young athlete reaches his junior or senior year in high school, that he approach the selection of a school and its athletic program as a career choice that will affect his vocational career as well. Above all, the athlete should be comfortable and happy with the sport in which he or she is participating.

Very few characteristics reflect better on a prospect than to be a second or third generation student-athlete. Coaches look upon pedigreed athletes favorably because they assume that the athlete is at least, well schooled in the fundamentals of the sport. Athletes who have the good fortune of having a former collegiate athlete in their family should heed any advice and direction given. It's important however, to stay away from the pressure of following in another's footsteps for the sake of family honor.

Probably the greatest decision my father ever made concerning my young athletic development was to keep me away from organized football. Although youth teams are organized by weight, as well as age, the likelihood of serious injury (i.e. a fracture to a growth region) was too much of a risk. I mention this only so parents understand that they should exercise control over the sport in which their child will participate. Know the risks involved for your youth before you consent to anything. Fortunately, my father allowed me to compete in high school football. As it turned out, football was one of the sports in which I was most recruited.

While it may be true that many athletes that have become great, achieved their greatness in one sport, most of these athletes did not specialize until their mid to late teens. In fact, a survey of 63 Olympic athletes revealed that only five ever specialized in just one sport before the age of twelve (Wolff, 1991). These results are fairly consistent with those found in professional team sports such as football, hockey and basketball.

There are many theories which attempt to explain the pitfalls of specialization. I firmly believe that a young athlete will work and excel in a sport in which he has experienced fun in both the game and practice situations. The more successes a young athlete has at practice, the greater his chances of success in actual competition, and vice versa.

The average student-athlete does not need to specialize until he reaches the college level. It is at the college level that the competition is most fierce, the demands to win are great, the academic pressures are immense, and social time is at a minimum.

Parental Expectations

As a youth coach, I know how easy it is for well intentioned parents to want to get involved in their youth's sport career. However parents expectations of their child's abilities may often exceed the coach's perceptions of the youth's abilities. In cases where the youth may not be getting the playing time expected, the youth should be encouraged (not the parent) to talk to the coach to see what is needed of him to get more time. Sometimes an agreement can not be made with the coach. In such cases, often, the athlete is better off seeking more playing time with a lessor skilled team rather than staying on the bench with a better team (especially pre-high school athletes).

Additional Suggestions

The following are some additional activities you may consider for your youth to pursue as he or she develops athletically.

Martial Arts

I can't say enough about the virtues of the martial arts, particularly karate. I believe every young student-athlete should have considerable exposure to karate or a similar art form during the formative years (5-13 years old).

I recommend karate to parents because the child is immediately exposed to the concepts of athletics, discipline, and confidence. For instance, the use of the belt system (a system by which achievement and skill are measured) is a great confidence builder for youngsters. The use of both the right and left sides of the body to complete exercises and drills enhances balance, and agility. The importance of concentration, discipline, and study, are required in order for one to ascend to the next rank (youngsters instinctively understand the work ethic and its virtues). Flexibility, power and strength are enhanced through calisthenic exercises and drills. In addition, the youth will learn self-defense, restraint and humility.

Weight Training v. Calisthenics

Strength is a very important factor in determining the level of an athlete's success. Resistance training is the most common form of strength training. For young athletes, resistance training, using one's body weight, will achieve strength goals without substantially increasing risk of personal injury. Calisthenic exercises such as push-ups, pull-ups, dips, sit-ups, calf raises, knee bends, stair/hill climbing, and running are just some of the many exercises which improve strength, power, speed, endurance, and stamina (see the appendix for more information). These exercises can be conducted with little or no supervision and without extensive investments in equipment.

As a general rule I would discourage youth under fifteen from using free weights without first having employed the suggested calisthenic exercises. The possibility of injury due to poor training and supervision is greater than that of calisthenics. In addition, many young athletes may be intimidated by some of the more developed lifters. In turn, overuse injuries may result as the younger athletes strive for quick results.

Sports Camps & Training Schools

If at all possible, send your youth to a sport camp or a training school (preferably one with housing accommodations). Some schools will even accommodate whole teams (and the coach). The opportunity to learn and experience a different point of view may benefit the athlete for life.

Training Schools and Camps offer athletes many opportunities to learn and get the recognition they deserve. However, not all schools and camps are equal. Some training schools can facilitate all aspects of a sport (i.e. all positions—offensive and defensive). Others may specialize on one position or aspect of a particular sport. Each offers a specific advantage. However, schools which provide instruction in addition to competitive play give an athlete an advantage over those schools which only simulate actual situations.

Many sports camps are not accredited, but are very good nonetheless. Prior to selecting a camp, get information on the staff and their background, the facilities, insurance coverage, the sessions, and the number of years in business.

A training school is generally concerned with focusing on the mission of improving the athlete's skills giving little regard to the extracurricular interests. Many of these schools are well represented with professional staff and college recruiters.

Athletic camps have a more relaxed atmosphere about them. Their focus on learning may be just as strong as that of training schools, but they can accommodate extracurricular interests far more easily. These camps are generally overnight camps and will be well represented with professional staff. In all fairness it is very difficult to say which is better, training schools or camps. The selection should be based on the long-term benefit received.

Recruitment Opportunity

Does this camp present a realistic recruiting opportunity? Is the staff representative of the types of college programs in which you have an interest? If the camp does not have strong representation, are written performance evaluations (or performance ratings) given?

Competition

Is there fair representation of athletes from outside your immediate area? Many camps have a strong reputation that enables them to attract national and international athletes. The advantage is that you have a mental picture of the types of athletes you are competing against for scholarships. Very quickly you will find out how good you really are—your weaknesses and strengths. In addition, camps present opportunities for you to make new friends. Perhaps you can share training routines, tips, and other mutually useful information. Other issues to consider are:

Experienced Instruction

Is the staff experienced in handling youth? What are their credentials?

Realistic Playing Conditions

Are playing conditions, similar to what an athlete would expect outside the training facilities? Is the field of play regulation?

Performance Evaluations

Are player evaluations given? Are these evaluations fair and accurate assessments of ability? Are athlete's strengths and weaknesses made known to them during the course of the week and corrected?

Duration

Is the camp a sleep over or day camp? Does the camp meet its objectives in the time frame?

Individual Attention

Will individual attention be given to each youth? What is the student/counselor ratio?

Cost

Is the cost of the camp or school a value, or are you paying for someone's reputation?

Selecting and Evaluating Youth Coaches

A youth coach (pre-high school) plays an important role in the development of an athlete. Unfortunately, the role of a youth coach is taken for granted. Many youth coaches believe that winning is the only goal to be achieved by playing a sport. Stay away from these types of "winning is the only thing" types because the goals are too shortsighted. Winning should be a more important issue after some mastery of skills and athleticism is attained (at the all-star, high school, college and pro levels).

During the formative years (pre-high school) the emphasis should be on having fun within a learning environment. A good youth coach will develop a rapport with the youth through his knowledge of the sport. If the coach is an individual who can demonstrate the skills, all the better. Self-motivation is the key to progress. The best coaches tend to self-motivate their "pupils."

Parental Influence is significant

Always know what is going on in your young athletes life, even if you can't get involved.

Always be positive about your youths performance. Always be constructive about what was done right in a loss. Minimize criticism. Let the young athlete decide what sport he or she would like to play and be supportive.

Dual and Triple Sport Management

Odds are great that, a collegiate athlete, will participate in only one sport (even if the athlete participated in more than one in high school). The reason for the concentration is practicality. The primary cause of this concentration is time, or lack of it. The collegiate academic challenges are, on average, greater than the average high school student-athlete has experienced. In addition to the academic demands, collegiate athletics, during the regular season, can have the equivalent burden of a part-time job (or a a full-time job at some institutions).

Assess the Commonalties

If you direct your child to compete, and compete well in two sports, you have to understand what is common among these sports in the way of skills, and athletic ability. For instance, a baseball player picking up tennis as a second sport, is involved in two sports which strongly complement one another. In fact, because they so strongly complement one another, there may be an opportunity to transfer some skills from one sport to the other.

Master the Fundamental Skills of Each New Sport

Just as a primary (or first) sport requires an understanding and commitment to learning the fundamentals, so to does the second sport require the same commitment. The benefit in playing a complementary sport is the smaller time frame in which new skills are learned. For example, the tennis forehand and backhand may be learned easily by a baseball athlete with a strong batting background. However, additional work on ground strokes may be needed as hitting for accuracy in baseball is not as critical as it is in tennis.

Off-season Pick-up Games Can Improve Skills

On occasion the young athlete will get the itch to play his primary sport during the later of the regular season of the secondary sport. As a way of re-learning the skills, ahtletes are first encouraged to compete in unorganized ("pick-up") type games against lessor skilled athletes. Of course, these pick-up games are not available in all sports. In those cases, encourage practice at about fifty to sixty percent intensity.

Work on the Precise Athletic Movements Last

As adjustment from the primary sport takes place, concentrate on rudimentary skills and movements–back to basics. Fortunately, the time frame in which one begins to adjust to an old style will be small. For example, use the first two weeks, of a six week program, to work on the basics. The remaining time could be used to develop additional skills.

Document The Current Conditioning Level

Prior to beginning any new training program, it is important to document the present conditioning level, skill level, and overall routine in a training journal. Documentation should include all objective measures (i.e. time, distance, weight, speed, etc.) and all subjective measures (i.e. played consistent, or within his abilities today).

Always Manage the Diet

Eating behavior should be managed, whether in training or not. This means that you want to monitor a sensible, well balanced diet, not one loaded with excess sugars (empty calories) and fats.

Take two weeks off from athletics to get the "itch" back.

After a tough season, It's generally good to take at least two weeks off, totally devoid of sports. The physical and mental rest will have a therapeutic effect and build a "fire" within, so that training may be effectively renewed.

Complementary Sports

The table on this page, is a guide to complementary sport(s). Don't worry if the sports in which you have an interest are not on the list. Dual or triple sport athletes do not have to compete in complementary sports in order to excel. Our list recognizes that there are strong characteristics in some sports which can be transferred to others fairly easily. There is no "true" complementary sport, but the characteristics to look for when deciding on a second or third sport are:

1) Fun
2) Complements existing Skills, Abilities, and Conditioning
3) Risk of Injury is Minimized
4) Conflict of Schedule is Minimized
5) Scholarship Opportunity

Table of Complementary Sports

FOOTBALL	BASKETBALL	SOCCER
Wrestling	Soccer	Cross Country
Track & Field	Track & Field	Track & Field
Basketball	Volleyball	
TRACK & FIELD	SWIMMING	HOCKEY
Volleyball	Track & Field	Basketball
Basketball	Cross Country	Track & Field
	Rowing	Wrestling
TENNIS	GOLF	VOLLEYBALL
Baseball	Swimming	Basketball
Track & Field	Tennis	Track & Field
Soccer		
WRESTLING	LACROSSE	BASEBALL
Track & Field	Track & Field	Basketball
Rowing	Tennis	Track & Field
	Basketball	Tennis
	Baseball	

Chapter Two

Self Inventory

To reach any goal, it is vitally important to have an understanding of "self." For example, do you prefer urban or country living? Have you decided on a college major? Do you prefer a large school or a small school? Do you want to stay close to home or live on-campus? These and many other questions will need to be answered prior to your pursuing a college athletic and academic career. For our purposes, a self-inventory is a personal list of wants, needs, skills, abilities, preferences, and traits used to evaluate a career track. Following are some suggestions as to how you will go about conducting your self-inventory.

1) **Be honest with yourself.** Be assured that a coach or recruiter will want to know why you are interested in their program. It is easier for both you and the coach to come to a final decision if there is a clear understanding of what each of you have to offer the other. Through this process, do not be afraid to evaluate and periodically reevaluate yourself and your

progress. Your goal is to determine what you want to do, and where you want to be for four years of your life. With this process include your goals, abilities, and most importantly your DESIRE! At least write those three items down (and include how you will achieve them).

If you're a male under eighteen you may expect to keep growing until your early twenties. Most women under the age of twenty have stopped growing. For youth who have not entered high school yet there are tests that can "predict", with a good amount of certainty, your future height. A qualified orthopedic surgeon will be able to administer this examination and explain the expectations for growth and development.

At least yearly, (and certainly before you begin any exercise program) have a physical examination conducted--a Prepartcipation Fitness Exam is recommended as its purpose is to ascertain overall fitness and health (Kibler, 1990). A physical is required in college and is normally performed by the institution. Are you completely injury free? Are your muscles proportionately balanced? Or could you use some more development in isolated areas? Are you maintaining a healthy diet? Are you taking any prescribed medication properly?

Next, and most important, should come an assessment of your academics. How are your grades? Are they average, or above average? If your grades are below a C (2.0) average you can improve (see chapter 7). How much do you know about your sport? Do you know the rules of your sport? Are you aware of the latest changes? Are you a student of the game? It is very important to know the rules and to be able to make decisions on them by instinct.

How competitive are you? Are you competitive to the point that you have to win or improve upon your personal best, every time? Maybe you are competitive to the point where most of the things you do, you improve upon from your last performance. Do you compete and work as hard in practice as you do in games? Does you enthusiasm and work ethic pass on to your teammates?

Do you push yourself to be better tomorrow than you are today? Do you learn from your mistakes? Once you are aware of your mistakes do you repeat them? If you lose a game do you learn from it? Do you understand why? Can you interpret the statistics of the game to find your opponents weaknesses? Re-examine the questions that I have asked and answer this one...Do you enjoy your sport? Be knowledgeable, be intense, be competitive and be well balanced!

2) **Set realistic goals**. If it is your desire to be a world class sprinter, expect that you'll have to be in pretty good shape to accomplish this. Being over weight, out of practice and out of condition will not help you in your drive to be the best you can be. Set goals that are easy to reach as well as challenging.

3) **Persevere through the lean times**. Skills and abilities improve with time. A growth spurt or exposure to a new way of doing things may open your eyes to a whole new world. Do not be afraid of setting too high a standard for yourself. Studies have shown that we are often our own worst critic. I remember the disappointment in not starting on my AAU basketball team while I was in high school. I was determined to do more than make the team, I wanted to start. The first opportunity I had to play, I put my personal feelings aside so the team could advance. I knew that if I played unselfishly on offense and concentrated on my responsibilities on defense we would win. Fortunately, my plan worked. I played the rest of that game and started the rest of the season.

4) **Praise yourself often for your achievements**. The psychological benefit can be tremendous. Constant positive reinforcement sets the stage for future successes. On occasion, you might want to treat yourself after achieving a goal.

Assessment of the Basics

Over time, we have all developed a degree of mastery of a sport. As you approach a higher level of competition, you quickly find out how adept you are in your sport. Scholastic, sport specific and extracurricular skills come together to paint a picture of the contributions you can make to an athletic program.

Scholastic Success

Your collegiate athletic career hinges more upon your academic performance than upon athletic performance. A recruiter is more inclined to make an offer to a student-athlete who has a 3.0 grade point average, athletic skills that can be developed and tremendous desire, than he would a superstar athlete with a 1.8 grade point average. Odds are, the less accomplished student-athlete will sit out the first year, lose a year of eligibility, or be declared ineligible before the third year.

Your scholastic ability is judged by your grades, standardized test scores or both. It is crucial that you accurately consider your scholastic abilities. If there are areas in which you need help, make sure that they are addressed now. Or, make sure that the institution which you plan to attend has the resources to accommodate your academic needs.

Sports Achievement

Sports achievement can be assessed in basically three ways: (1) personal best, (2) relative to the competition, or (3) relative to existing records. Achievement based upon personal best, occurs in sports such as baseball (i.e., batting average or earned run average) or golf (i.e. handicap). In cases where an assessment is made, evaluations can be misleading. Frequently athletes show promise by improving upon personal skills, only to falter against more highly skilled athletes. However, personal gains are always encouraging as they indicate consistency. You will be able to position your level of achievement in to one of the three categories.

For most team sports, sport achievement relative to competition is the most significant. For example, soccer requires that many skills be mastered (dribbling, passing, shooting, etc.). Although these skills may not show up on the stat sheet, they are immediately recognizable by the trained eye. As you get older you may find that being the best in your little corner of the world, may not mean you are "the" best. Mastery of the skills is one of the most vital links to receiving an athletic scholarship. Measure your skill level honestly. Get a second and even third opinion from a coach or teammate. Do you now possess the fundamental skills of a collegiate student-athlete?

We suggest, as a minimum average, a collegiate athlete will score, an eight or higher, on four of seven fundamental skill levels, in his or her position or sport, to virtually guarantee a scholarship offer. Notice however that each sport has its own standard of fundamental skills. For example, higher skill and technique sports such as golf, or track may require an athlete to possess more skills (i.e. one set of fifteen skills) with each skill having relatively little impact upon overall performance. Whereas football, requires mastery of a few skills and a high degree of athleticism. Look at the following table labeled "Soccer Skill Matrix." Notice, we have isolated seven essential skills that would be sought after by a collegiate coach. With the assistance of an experienced coach, my skill level was determined and the result was used to assist in the selection process. I was not an All-American, All-State, or All County selection. Yet, I received a full athletic scholarship at an NCAA Division II school, as a defender, by properly assessing my skills.

Soccer Skill Matrix

Skills	Prospect	H.S. All State/Cnty	H.S. All-American	Collegian
1. Trapping	9	8	9.5	7-10
2. Passing	8	8	9.5	7-10
3. Dribbling	7	8	9.5	7-10
4. Defending	9	8	9.5	7-10
5. Scoring	5	8	9.5	7-10
6. Shooting	7	8	9.5	7-10
7. Heading	9	8	9.5	7-10
Total	54	56	66.5	49

Extracurricular Activities

In what extracurricular activities do you now participate? Would you like to continue to participate in them in college? What skills have you learned from these activities? Can those skills be applied to your sport? For example, do not underestimate your student government activities, or your participation in a school club. Your involvement could demonstrate the leadership skills always sought after by recruiters.

Ability

Do not confuse skills with abilities. A simple definition of ability is; the application of skill. To illustrate, examine again the Soccer Skill Matrix. Throughout my high school career, I was used to playing in the midfield (the position requires offensive and defensive skills). Notice, however, my skill level scores of dribbling and scoring, two important offensive requirements, were relatively weak by college standards. It was true that I had those skills but it was not true that I possessed the *ability* to use those skills comfortably on offense. My ability to use the skills I possessed was better suited for defense. The level of skill did not change but the surroundings in which I used them did. The mark of a team or individual to adapt to a new challenge is *ability*. Any recruiter or coach in the country can evaluate skill. Ability can only be determined by the individual in the way he reacts to competition and challenges.

Athletic ability is judged by your success against the competition. Have you demonstrated the ability to get the victory in the last second? Have you been able to get the victory by running the anchor leg? Are you the person the team goes to when the game is on the line? Are you able to make the seven foot putt for the win? These are abilities that attract coaches and recruiters-excellence under pressure!

Knowledge

Knowledge of your sport is critical. Familiarity of the rules of the game, and the constant changes that effect the game is necessary if you are going to compete in college. Part of the college experience is the ever unceasing need to learn and to keep abreast of the competition. Who amongst your sport is considered the premier player? More importantly, why? Study and know the rules of your sport. Watch film often to learn from players who are more and less skilled.

Further, knowledge of strategy, and more importantly, when and where to apply certain strategies is quite important. Some of the knowledge in a particular sport comes through direct competition. Knowledge of a particular sport can also come from observing the professionals of your sport and by observing game film.

Coaching styles vary as much as individual personalities. Do the skills you possess match with your prospective coaches individual philosophy. Have you scouted your prospective school's team? Are you aware of its strengths and weaknesses and what you perceive your role to be once you are on the team? Athletic teams will normally take on the personality of the coach. If a team has a style to which you would feel comfortable playing, most likely you and the coach will get along very well.

Seize Opportunities

Knowledge of your sport and of your own abilities is important. Within almost every sport, and certainly most team sports, weaknesses and strengths become readily apparent. Take time to characterize your style. Do you function better by instinct and impulse as opposed to deliberate and calculated action? Think about your style carefully. This step is important as to your development and in targeting schools in your particular sport. In your study of prospective schools, maybe you will find a few that have a possible opening in your position. Often information can be gathered by contacting your prospective schools athletic department's Sports Information Office by collecting a program or roster for your review. Opportunities sometimes arise as the result of a rebuilding process, or as a result of a coaching change. For example, you may notice that one of your targeted schools is losing three senior defenders. Another school may be hiring a coach you have known since 10th grade summer camp.

The Generalist

As a rule, the generalist has the greater chance of receiving a scholarship. It is the generalist who can contribute in many different ways. The more "weapons" (actual skills and abilities) you offer to a prospective school the greater your chances of landing a full scholarship. For example, a soccer player that can play any position on the field, is likely to have more options available to him than another athlete that can play only one. Of course if you play one position better than any of your peers you are certainly at a greater advantage. Actual game experience in these positions can sometimes be very weighty in making close scholarship decisions. In addition, an athlete who plays more than one sport also increases his chances of receiving a scholarship.

Being a regular starter on a varsity team does have its advantages, but starting does not mean that a scholarship is automatic. There are many high school athletic programs, across the country, in many sports, that annually place their starters and non-starting seniors in athletic programs with full scholarships. After all, if everyone had to be a starter to get a college scholarship, there would not exist a player called the "sub." At some high school athletic programs starting is an automatic birth to the college level. Getting an offer to an institution is largely determined by the success of the program and the coach behind it. In other words, its all relative. It's not out of the question that a four year varsity starter on the volleyball team in Maine get overlooked for a substitute from a very strong California program. California is very rich scouting territory for that sport. Each region of the country has its own particular strengths and weaknesses in its respective sports.

Wants

Sometimes getting what we want comes down to the act of asking. Take time to consider your best case scenario. Outline a plan that allows for your perfect situation, your least perfect situation and everything in between. In the following discussions, we have taken the issue of academic competition as an issue by which your school selection is based.

The highly competitive academic programs, generally have the most stringent academic requirements. These schools may require extraordinarily more study, class participation, and involvement than average. Sports participation does not usually garner extra sympathy or patience from a professor or classmates for missed assignments or homework. The students at these schools have high grade point averages and high standardized test scores. They rank among the top in their class and have a history of academic awards and honors. Entrance requirements of the students are the most selective.

Some moderately competitive schools may not rank amongst the most elite, but they may be fairly selective about their new applicants. Students will normally have above average grades and standardized test scores. There is a fair amount of balance in campus life. The academic regimen is not as stringent as that of the most competitive schools. The instructors are good to excellent and you can expect to spend a lot of time in the library.

The least competitive schools will generally have open or non-selective admission requirements. The student population may represent a diverse cross-section of the population. The instructors are good as is the academic curriculum.   The curriculum often reflects the current needs of the state or locality.

Athletic Wants

If it is your ambition to appear on national television on Saturday, then you may have a desire to be a member of one the most competitive sports programs in the country.   These programs' coaches recruit the elite of athletic talent across the country. They have the resources to make the student-athlete's college experience exceed his or her greatest expectations. Some of these schools are just as intense about their academics as they are about their athletics.

Moderately competitive schools will regularly get the local news coverage and will have strong name recognition. All the athletes will not be blue-chippers, but they will have formidable credentials. These schools are highly respected in their home state from which they draw a large amount of their talent. They may have walk-on tryouts annually, and may select a few of the athletes to play on varsity. They will generally participate in post-season play but will very often, lose in the earlier rounds.   They may compete against one or two programs recognized as the elite in their sport.

The least competitive schools normally fit a pattern. The programs, do not compete against the   most competitive schools. Their won-loss record will be average and they may even have a history of .500 or below seasons. They will probably have few to no blue-chippers throughout their program.

College life

The life that athletes lead outside of sports is just as important as the one involving sports. College offers diversity and freedom of choice. It is important to make careful decisions regarding your surroundings. If you are from a very strong rural setting, and plan to attend an urban school, take time to visit and understand your surroundings before making a move.

Urban schools with large student populations offer density and convenience. Access to facilities such as libraries, theaters, restaurants, attractions and the like, come in greater abundance. If you are an athlete who is used to receiving a lot of attention, you may be one amongst the crowd. High student to teacher ratios, some as high as three hundred to one, exist in basic core curriculum classes.

Urban colleges with small student populations may not offer the density or resources of the larger populated universities. You will feel a stronger sense of belonging and purpose at a less populated college. The student to teacher ratio may be one to which you are more accustomed if you are used to having regular contact with your instructor. Access to facilities such as libraries, theaters, restaurants, attractions and such are just as accessible as with the larger populated schools.

Rural colleges with large student populations normally offer a next-to-home type of environment. There may be one major avenue or highway which acts as the thoroughfare to shops, attractions, and points of interest. The culture is somewhat reserved but offers a welcome change from the big city. If you are from a big city and enjoy a festive night life you may be homesick from the change.

Representing the smallest of the smallest are the rural schools with small student populations (i.e. total student population under three thousand). These schools, though rich in academia offer few activities of interest outside of the regular academic environment (i.e. art, music, theater, sports). You may find that one or just a few industries dominate the area. There is little to no public transportation, and in most cases, a car is needed if you want to go to your place of interest. The people are friendly, respectful, reserved, and often conservative in their views.

Post-Collegiate Career

College presents many opportunities through which one can explore his interests and passions. However, some institutions are not able to offer the diversity of curriculum, exposure of culture, and the freedom of exploration. Certainly, the larger populated schools may offer the flexibility of choice because of their financial backing. Weigh your athletic choices with your career choices and vice versa. If you are not sure what your career choices are you may want to attend a university or college that offers diversity and exposure to different cultures. If you feel strongly about your career objectives then you will want to attend the school that will provide you with the skills, training, and exposure you need to stand out amongst the crowd. There are trade-offs to be made for attending the school of your choice. Nothing is permanent, and certainly no one will ever blame you for doing what is in your best interest.

Make sure that the college or university of your choice has a track record of successful placement of its graduates. Check with the particular offices responsible for maintaining such data. Find out about work study programs that can provide you with income during the summer months, college credit, and valuable experience.

Keep in mind, to attend a school out-of-state has certain disadvantages when it comes to job placement. Although many institutions provide job placement assistance, the facilities and even the majority of the jobs for which it is trying to place will reside in-state or within a specified area. So if you plan on going to State University of Montana, don't expect too much job placement assistance once you move back to your home state of New York.

Needs

Our next discussion involves you personally evaluating issues to determine your needs. Do not take these issues and activities lightly. Your college experience should be positive and one that you will be able to happily reflect upon for the rest of your life. Your mental state of mind and sense of comfort will directly effect your academic and athletic performance. Although a coach may not take away a scholarship due to athletic performance they can often make your life very complicated.

Scholastic Needs

Student-athletes who have a need to study in a highly competitive academic environment are generally those students with a solid history of academic success. To study in this environment, and survive, will definitely detract from your athletic commitments. Determine beforehand from your coach, what the pre-season and regular season practice schedules are like. At some schools, during the regular season, you may practice a minimum of twenty hours a week. It is not unheard of for a program to maintain practice sessions which are each up to three hours long. Depending upon one's major and course load, it is possible for a student-athlete to maintain a 7:00 am to 12:00 am daily schedule.

When you are a scholarship student-athlete the coaches and support staff may tell you that your books come first, but remember it is the scholarship that is paying your way. Missing practices can be grounds for rescission of your scholarship. Intense courses, those which include vast amounts of daily homework, should be taken outside of the regular season where practices, games and travel do not interfere.

Generally provisions within both the NCAA and NAIA allow for the continuation of aid even after academic graduation. For instance, if you were to complete your study in three years instead of four, the university or college is obligated to award you a grant-in-aid for the fourth year. So if graduate school is on your list then you may be giving yourself a slight financial advantage by finishing early.

Moderately competitive schools offer great academic value without some of the name recognition you would find from the most competitive colleges. Do not underestimate their caliber of instruction or their level of its diversity.

Your academic challenges can be fulfilled at one of these schools. If name recognition, after graduation, is what you seek, then these schools offer a credible record of performance and contribution that the local and non-local communities will recognize.

If you are going to make an assumption about a school don't make the assumption that schools with less competitive entrance requirements give out degrees. Colleges and universities are accredited. If you attend a school that is not accredited then you are wasting your time, because any degree from an unaccredited school is worthless. The majority of the lessor competitive schools will be the state schools. If you need a sense of security, you may want to send in an application so that you have a fall-back position. Your chances of acceptance at one of these schools strongly increases if it is an in-state school.

Sports Needs

If you come from an intensely competitive sports background, don't sell yourself short. You will need to compete in an environment that is developing and challenging. If you have come from an area where your sport is "king" and everything comes to a halt on game day, then you owe it to yourself to pursue the best program. If you have always wondered what it is like to play in a big arena, on TV, or in front of large crowds then your need would be fulfilled at a high-profile/competitive program. Schools in the NCAA Division-I offer the best amateur competition in the nation. Many athletes that participate at this level have career related ambitions as professional players or coaches.

Though not as competitive as the NCAA's premiere division, NCAA division II programs, NAIA programs, and certain NJCAA programs offer challenging and moderately competitive sports. You may recognize many former all-america, all-state, or all-county high school performers now on the rosters of these schools. Fewer athletes in these divisions pursue professional ambitions in their sport than in the more competitive NCAA D-I. Some athletes will move on to four-year schools (as is the case for NJCAA athletes). Many look at the athletic competition as a means to receiving an education they may otherwise not be able to afford.

All the benefits, (room, board, tuition and books) exist at these programs (except at commuter schools) as they do at the higher division, however, they may exist on a more modest scale. Your competitive and academic needs can be met here, though the name recognition may not be as readily apparent.

The lessor profile/competitive schools meet the needs of student-athletes whose athletic involvement is truly secondary. Athletic programs at these colleges and universities are maintained mostly for namesake and status over that of funding sports dynasties. If you were an all-state selection looking to attain a degree with little distraction, you will, athletically, be able to coast through the regimen. Schools perennially at or near the bottom of the division or conferences, coaches with less than or near .500 records and tenure, are good signs that they may be receptive to what you have to offer.

Chapter Three

The College Game

Recruiting athletes to the college ranks is an art form which many coaches have mastered. If you wonder how seemingly marginal athletes get scholarships you must first understand recruiting policies.

College coaches distribute awards based on their athletic budget. A majority of the student athletes on almost any collegiate team will be in-state students. The reason, a scholarship award of an out-of-state student can be double the award for an in-state student. From a financial-aid point of view, awarding as many in-state scholarships as possible, effectively gives the coach more money to spend on his program. If the coach has more money available he can plan more trips, recruit harder, and build a stronger program. Of course this scenario does not develop at institutions where the tuition and related expenses are the same for out-of-state students. As a result, your scholarship search should begin in-state, especially if you desire to attend a two-year community college prior to attending a four-year school.

Eligibility

Our first assumption regarding your eligibility is you are now or were formerly a student athlete between the age of nine and eighteen. If you are already in college, we'll assume that you have at least two years of athletic eligibility remaining, prior to your graduation.

We'll also assume that your ambition is to compete in intercollegiate athletics in either one of the following associations:

NAIA (National Association of Intercollegiate Athletics)

NCAA (National Collegiate Athletic Association)

NJCAA (National Junior College Athletic Association).

Our next assumption regarding your eligibility is you meet all of the academic requirements of one of the aforementioned associations. Further, you should meet the requirements for maintaining athletic eligibility. The two are not necessarily the same. For instance you could be a straight "A" student but still be athletically ineligible. If, you do not practice as required by your coach then you may become athletically ineligible to keep your scholarship. If you become athletically ineligible or academically ineligible you either lose the scholarship you do have or you do not qualify to receive a scholarship. It is the combination of academic and athletic eligibility that determines whether or not you may receive an offer or keep your award.

Eligibility represents the most confusing and troubling aspect of collegiate athletics. Many governing bodies play a role in influencing eligibility. These groups include high school associations, collegiate conferences, individual institutions and major governing bodies such as the NCAA, NAIA, and NJCAA. College eligibility is determined before one enters a college or university, therefore it can be seriously jeopardized while in high school. It is beyond the scope of this book to answer eligibility questions and concerns for every individual situation and circumstance. However, you would put yourself at risk by not knowing general provisions. We have developed some criteria to keep in mind which, when followed, may allow for safe passage through the amateurism and eligibility maze.

Eligibility covers, in its basic form, academics, personal contact, athletic participation, endorsement/sponsorship, and amateurism. We cover these elements in general. For specific information, we recommend that you pursue consultations with a knowledgeable counselor or coach and the latest regulatory manual. You should safely surpass all eligibility tests if you follow the basic steps we prescribe. Eligibility standards and policies change almost every year.

(1) **Academics**: Minimally, a student-athlete seeking an athletic scholarship should maintain a cumulative grade point average *above* 2.5 (on a 4.0 scale). The core curriculum of the state and of the prospective schools should be adhered. Notice that even if you meet the core curriculum guidelines of your state, or graduate from high school, it is possible that you may not meet some entrance guidelines for certain colleges and universities. Such a result may occur, if for example, you attended a vocational school. If it is your goal to pursue a college education you should be taking a pre-college level curriculum. A good score on a standardized test, such as the SAT (above 900), should make you appealing to many schools. In addition to standardized test scores, is the in-class performance. If you maintain a strong B average you will open up many doors.

(2) **Personal contact**: If you make any contact before your junior year with a coach or perspective school it should be through coincidence at a sports camp. Refrain from phone conversations, letters, and visits, contact made with parents, guardians or siblings, or anything else which might be construed as a direct or indirect contact. Your athletic eligibility is at stake just as much as an athletic program's reputation and good standing. In some cases, you may not only jeopardize your collegiate eligibility, but your high school eligibility as well, because some high school associations will intervene on matters of eligibility. Different sports maintain standards and these standards could get even more complicated if you play more than one sport. As always, seek professional, or well informed counseling. Your athletic director, coach, and the college athletic association of interest can be of help.

(3) **Amateurism**:   Amateur status is the corner stone of collegiate athletic competition. The status can be easily lost by participating in some of the most, seemingly, harmless events. To stand clear of complications, (a) Never talk to anyone who enlists their services to represent you in any athletic capacity-no agents (b) Never compete in any professionally endorsed or sponsored event (i.e. The Widget Co. Slam Dunk competition). Do not accept air fares, travel accommodations, etc. Simply, if prize money, future financial considerations, endorsements and the like are involved, you do not want to go near them. Many student athletes have permanently lost their eligibility for seemingly innocent infractions.

(4) **Endorsement/Sponsorship**: Never lend your name to any product or promotion arranged for the purpose of transacting business. This includes autograph signings or scheduled appearances at the local drugstore. Many athletes have jeopardized their eligibility by innocently attending certain corporate sponsored events (i.e. some all-star games). Be sure you are aware of the consequences before you participate in the events.

Recruitment

The following sports have been selected as our core selection. These sports are fairly well represented in high school and college. This list should not be considered absolute as there are sports not included on this list for which scholarships are available: Football, Basketball, Baseball, Cross Country, Hockey, Soccer, Lacrosse, Tennis, Track & Field, Volleyball, Wrestling, Swimming /Diving, Gymnastics, and Golf.

The techniques and information in this guide benefit student-athletes who fit into one of four categories:

1) A student-athlete who is a pre-high schooler (at least nine years old).
2) A student-athlete who is in high school but not a senior.
3) A student-athlete who is a high school senior.
4) A student-athlete prospect who is in college (walk-on).

The processes involving recruitment, publicity, play, and skill level vary greatly with each sport. A fair comparison at the college level, can not be made between, football, and golf. Golfers have handicaps, and are judged by their performance on courses which have varying levels of difficulty. A good golfer is judged solely by the score card. On the other hand, a football player primarily uses his physical attributes (height, weight, and speed, for example) and skill, along with the performance of supporting players. If he has a poor performance the team could compensate for his weak areas and still preserve a win, whereas a golfer is on his own.

Collegiate sports can also be separated by the revenue they produce. Team sports such as football, basketball, hockey, and baseball may produce high revenues for institutions. Post-season tournaments, television, gate revenues and, promotional sales (shirts, hats and the like) in these sports   may actually underwrite an institution's investment in its sports program. In many instances, winning a national title has been known to increase student enrollment.

In addition, there are those sports we call the quasi-team sports. These are the sports which allow for team and individual scoring as a means of determining wins, losses, and rankings (track and field, tennis, and gymnastics being such examples). For our purposes we will put these sports in the category of individual sports.   An individual who runs a 46 second 400 meter dash will get a scholarship regardless of the quality of the high school program. A gymnast who collects three perfect scores in a state competition will probably be high on the list of recruiters regardless of how the team finishes in the meet.

Individual sports are unique, in that there is only one person responsible for a win or a loss, the athlete. Generally, when a coach considers a track athlete they consider one of three things—"How fast...?", "How far...?", or "How high...?"

When a coach considers a track athlete they look at meet times relative to existing records, relative to head-to-head competition, and relative to personal bests. To get an offer the track athlete has to perform consistently in two of the three categories for a coach to take a chance on offering a scholarship. In some circles the recruiter will also consider family history. However, a coach is interested in objective figures.

Sports in which judgment directly determines scoring, can inhibit an athletes opportunities to receive his due recognition. Gymnastics is a sport which falls in this category as scoring is largely affected by order of appearance. Some topics discussed will not necessarily apply to the sport, but on the whole you will benefit from many of our recruiting, training, publicity and other techniques we present.

A point worth noting is the fact that some sports, such as tennis,   rely upon the level of competition pursued.   An individuals ranking and head-to-head wins and losses greatly shape how he or she will approach or be approached by an institution for an athletic scholarship. To a larger extent the coaching one has received may play a factor in the recruitment process.

The life of a student athlete is filled with many honors and privileges, but living expenses is not one of them. Before accepting a scholarship to a school in an area unfamiliar to you, understand your living expense costs. These costs may include items such as toiletries, clothes, entertainment, transportation (to and from school), dating, phone service, laundry, unexpected school supply expenses.

It's a fact that your athletic talent has a value. That value is the cost of tuition, room, and board at a university or college for which you are given a scholarship. For some, this annual value could be as little as four thousand, or as much as twenty thousand dollars per year. Normally, the value of the athletic package will reflect the academic and athletic program of the university or college of your choice.

Understand the process regarding the recruitment of student athletes at the school for which you have an interest. Many schools have budgets which do not allow them to view talents outside a certain geographical area. Maybe they will accept film, or attend a camp, or sporting event in which you will (or can) participate. Sometimes you may have to take the first steps towards receiving an offer for an athletic scholarship.

Seven Keys To Success.

Evaluating talent is not an exact science. However, there are seven common qualities recruiters consider when they evaluate talent.

The foremost quality a recruiter looks for is *Ability*. A good college prospect will be able to demonstrate his raw talent that allows him to thrive at the high school level. In addition, the recruiter seeks to find glimpses of an athletes potential to elevate his talents to the more competitive collegiate level.

Next, a recruiter will look at the *Skills* of an athlete. Mastery of the fundamentals is of key concern. However, athleticism can compensate for lapses in skill because many coaches believe that athleticism can not be taught.

Another quality recruiters look for in a collegiate athlete is his *Knowledge* of the sport. Knowledge could include a combination of strategy, history, or experience.

Athleticism is the raw talent an athlete brings to the sport (i.e. power, strength, agility, etc.). Starting on page 47 we list nine basic athletic attributes.

The *Physique* of an athlete is of importance as many coaches recruit a certain body type which fits into a master plan. One's physique alone, depending upon the sport, can generate interest from recruiters.

Academic (scholastic) ability is of great concern to many recruiters as they want to be assured that a recruit maintains his eligibility throughout his or her college career.

Lastly the issue of *Character* is of importance because recruiters want to know if the recruit will fit in with fellow teammates. An athlete's character is reflected in his work ethic and general attitude.

In summary, these seven qualities are a basic check list. The degree of variety is strong. Some coaches may use a smaller set of criteria or may have a check list opposite of the one you see listed here. Not to worry. Your research of your prospective school will give you an indication of the proper mix for you.

Chapter Four

Personal Map

We spent a lot of time studying what you want and need on the personal level. Do not be afraid to wake up one morning and decide that some of your wants and needs have changed. Many young students change their mind as they are exposed to new experiences. Our purpose for the self-inventory was to place you at a starting point on your road to success in collegiate athletics. Throughout this chapter you will begin to formulate the execution phase of the plan. After reading this guide, you may want to track your progress and evaluate the results of your execution.

Set your objective

From the outset, we have stated what your final objective might be—to receive a full athletic scholarship and to start on varsity. Feel free to change the objective for your personal comfort level. Maybe you will want to concentrate on making the team for now.

Athletic Attributes

Your body's muscles are developed and used differently, sport to sport. Some sports require more distance, while others require more strength and speed. Regardless of the sport, you still must attain a base level of fitness to be successful. What type and combination of physical attributes does your sport demand? Determine from your experience and study, the most needed and utilized features. We suggest beginning with the nine attributes we have listed below. However the need of the attributes varies from sport to sport. For some sports (i.e. soccer, lacrosse and hockey) you may find that you will have to possess more of a balance of physical attributes to be successful. For other sports, i.e. football or basketball, you may find that you should possess higher than average concentrations of power, strength, and speed than all the other categories combined. Use the following tests if you compete in football, baseball, soccer, basketball, tennis, track and field, lacrosse, hockey, volleyball, wrestling, and field hockey and swimming:

1.) **Strength**: the ability to move resistance—time not a factor. For example the bench press is a strength test. You are testing how much weight (resistance) you can move, irregardless of how fast you move it. Test: bench press/deep squat max. at 2 reps or max. of push ups in one   set. Minimum Recommended: Bench Press- 2 reps at body weight; Squat-2 reps at 1.5 x body weight

2.) **Quickness**:   The ability to move in a limited time frame. Test: 10 yd. and back x 4.

3.) **Power**: The ability to move resistance within a specified time or space. Test: Vertical leap test (also known as jump and reach test) is a test of power.

4.) **Flexibility**:   The degree to which one's muscles are pliant. It is tested by measuring one's range of motion.   Recommendation: Stretching is the safest and effective means of achieving flexibility (refer to our reference section for a guide to stretching).

5.) **Agility**: The ability to move in a given direction, with dexterity, within a specified time. Test: Jump forward, then backward, then to the left, then to the right. Begin another cycle by jumping forward. Do this exercise for 30 seconds.

6.) **Stamina**:   Aerobic condition (aerobic means "with oxygen"). Stamina is the body's ability to provide the muscles with oxygen for an extended amount of time. Test: One mile run.

7.) **Endurance**:   The ability of muscles to perform their specific functions without succumbing to fatigue. Test: Push-ups or deep knee bends or exercises requiring high repetitions of muscle use.

8.) **Speed**: One's ability to put his full body in motion along an area, within a time frame. Test: 100 meter sprint.

9.) **Kinesthetic Awareness**: presence of mind ("sixth sense") to know and understand one's surroundings at any given point in time. This ability, mostly, comes by experience. For some, it is the ability to make a cut at the right time. For track athletes, it can be knowing when to begin your "kick" in the final lap.

General Sports Knowledge

Do you know the rules under which you play? The very basic level of knowledge should cover field or surface of play, its dimensions and end-markings, the number of participants, duration of play, the dimensions and limitations of any equipment used, rules governing player participation, the officials, any and all penalties and infractions, and the requirements to continue to the post-season.

Scouting collegiate programs in which you have an interest, involves monitoring teams over a regular period so you have a realistic idea of your chances to receive a scholarship. The process involves tracking the teams current won-loss record, verifying coaching staff information, researching the origin of the current recruits and their particular gifts examining the won-loss record for the past five years, the conference record, and any post-season play. If a junior college, examine how many of their athletes have gone on to four-year schools.

The information you gather should be used to determine trends which develop over time. A team's won-loss record could indicate how competitive it is. A strong record could indicate that recruitment is very serious and only athletes with strong credentials are considered. The frequency at which a team competes in the post-season can also be a sign of strength. The statistics you gather are only indications of possible interest in your abilities.

College Selection

Without a doubt, of the three, the NCAA is the most competitive association in the nation. Its constituents represent the best and finest academic and financial resources available. Second, competition wise, would have to be the NAIA. The NAIA represents collegiate competition without the tremendous fanfare and hype of the NCAA. The colleges are small, but the programs of study are all four-year programs. There are more than 500 member schools with over 65,000 scholarship athletes. Third is the NJCAA. It's junior college constituency represents a feeder system to the larger and more powerful NCAA and NAIA. There are national tournaments and ranking systems which record individual and group achievement.

Post-season events among NCAA member schools predominate in popularity with the American public. Divisions I and II provide events and tournaments to vie for national crowns, awards, and recognition. Some of these tournaments are the most popular amateur athletic sporting events in the nation. The hosts have been known to attract sell-out crowds. The NAIA and NJCAA also offer competitive and exciting post-season tournaments and events.

There is no real measure for gauging the quality of campus life. However, you will find that NAIA member schools are much smaller (in student population) schools on average than its NCAA counterparts. NJCAA schools are mostly "commuter" schools and will therefore rarely maintain any type of dormitory style arrangements. However, some assistance may be received for off-campus housing.

The regulatory maze one must adhere to can be a detractor with all associations. Be careful to meet the requirements for each sport. Though, in theory, no coach can take away a scholarship for athletic performance (or the lack of it) realize that all scholarships are technically issued, year-to-year.

Each year conference match-ups and tournaments bring about excitement and new life to the competitive spirit. Be it baseball, soccer, football, track, hockey, golf, or others, conference and inter conference rivalries attract attention.

While we would like to prototype the typical or ideal school situation for each athlete, the variety and magnitude of collegiate athletics prohibit the ambition. The very strength of collegiate athletics is choice. Always make the decision which benefits you the most academically, athletically, socially, vocationally, and emotionally.

When scouting your collegiate institutions be sure to discover the conferences to which they are members. Besides possibly finding schools which would be interested in your talents, you will discover some of the guidelines regarding eligibility and participation.

Formerly, but briefly, we covered the role of the coach and his influence on the decisions and actions you will make. Just as you scout a program and learn of its characteristics, so to, must the coaches themselves be scouted. An athletic program will usually take on the personality of its coach. If your final decision regarding your college selection significantly influenced upon the athletic program, select the program which you believe has the better coach.

There are many philosophies which explain how coaches act and react. We attempt to provide you with some of the behind-the-scenes information of which you may not be aware which, nonetheless, effect coaching behavior.

Coaching is a job. Some coaches feel that their job strictly involves winning games, and that's it. They conduct practices, they monitor player activity and win games in a fairly mechanical manner. Their career is often met with swings of highs and lows. Others may take a more involved approach, including coaching, advising, and nurturing. These coaches are prone to win the admiration and respect from their athletes based upon a sincere desire to win and be the best that they can be. Their routine is very structured, however they will provide their attention to even the lessor talented of the group.

There are coaches who believe that they have a special system. Their system is designed to suit the attributes and abilities of a certain type of student athlete. You can generally ascertain a coach's preference through his recruiting style. Coaches are usually very pattern oriented in their technique.

Once locked and determined about a certain style and type of athlete, they can rarely be persuaded otherwise. If recruiters come across a region which has generated successful athletes, they will tend to return to the area. Some will even monitor the recruiting practices and tendencies of their competition and target those areas for recruits. A famous case in point, involves the recruitment of Michael Jordan. He had an interest in a west coast school recognized for its basketball tradition. His interest in attending the school was strong. In fact, at the time, he was rated as one of the best players in the South. However, the coach at the university decided that he would not fit into their scheme! Michael's record speaks for itself.

There is another type of coach. This coach has a system developed, but tries to run the system with the talent available. Generally you will find that coaches which subscribe to this philosophy are generally the most open minded and receptive to the capabilities of new recruits. They are especially keen on recruits who can make multiple contributions to the team. These are generally the tendencies which you will encounter in coaches, and in their staffs. There are no particular set of guidelines, other than to follow your instincts. If you write to a coach or institution, do you get a timely response? Or, do you believe that your letter has hit the trash can the minute it arrived through the door? These are some of the tell tale signs of the organization and character of an athletic program.

Every year coaches, and athletic directors, sit down and discuss the previous season(s) and direction of the athletic programs in the new season. Coaches may address particular needs or particular concerns they have. Athletic directors (the coach's boss) may review graduation rates, rule changes, budgets, schedules, etc. These meetings and activities are done so that the athletic programs are in accord with the college's general purpose and mission.

Fact finding

Probably the most grueling aspect about making it to college is that you may not be sure how to make or begin making a match with the programs of your choice. Begin the process by grouping your prospects according to how you personally rank them (as determined by your personal investigation and interviews from knowledgeable sources):

(1) Definites
(2) Maybe so's
(3) Long-shots

Remember to look at your prospective schools achievements in the areas of academics and athletics.

Base you decision on issues that are important to you. Have confidence in the fact that you will come to a good decision based upon sound research and investigation.

It is always best to have a fall-back position to which you know you can turn. Maintain contact with the schools for which you know you definitely have a scholarship. It is better to have a scholarship at a small school than no scholarship at all. Pursue your "maybe so's and long-shots" vigorously but do not lose sight of the overall goal.

Chapter Five

Getting Noticed

If you expect to get an athletic scholarship, your reputation will precede you. The level of successful publicity you create, is the result of good practice habits, work ethic, scholastic performance, character, physical attributes, skill and performance on the field. In short, a student-athlete has the power to create his or her own publicity!

Before executing any plan you should know, who, and what, your support system consists. Use any number of these resources for assistance when you need them. Never be afraid to ask for help.

Your resources for assistance

Coaches: Do not underestimate the contribution · your coach can make to your collegiate athletic career. As a matter of fact, very few college coaches will recruit a student-athlete without a consultation with a high school coach. The value in making such a contact, is to determine the athletes character, work habits, and potential for success at the collegiate level. If you initiate contact between yourself and a collegiate coach, a follow-up is sure to include your high school coach. Be sure to maintain a healthy relationship with your coach. Many high school coaches today, have had playing experience at the college level. Coaches may give you the inside track on an athletic scholarship.

Guidance Counselors: Counselors offer the assistance you may need in the way of college selection and more. Their assistance can range from counseling on academic curriculum to coordinating vocational assistance.

Teachers: By far, teachers are the most underutilized resource of the average student-athlete. Teachers are available to help with your academic issues (remember that more than half of your athletic scholarship is dependent upon academic performance). Use them to assist you in improving on study techniques, test taking skills, and managing your academic load. Most teachers are very responsive to questions and concerns that you may have about your academic career.

Former student-athletes: Former athletes give you the benefit of knowing, first-hand, what the actual student-athlete experience is about. Your coaches may be able to put you in contact with them. They are a great resource to access if you plan on attending their alma mater. When gathering information from them, make sure that you stick with the facts. Ask open-ended questions about the program. How were the student athletes treated? What types of resources were provided to them for academic, medical, and athletic support? What is the coaching staff like? During the regular season what is the practice schedule like?

Training Partners: Training partners offer motivation and support. The relationship that should be attained should be built upon mutual goals. Your training partner may want to get an athletic scholarship just as badly as you do. Your skill level should be fairly close to your partner's. The greatest value in having a training partner is that you are motivated to support each other. There is something about the human condition that restricts us from disappointing another person. A true and loyal partner will push you further than you thought possible.

Parents: Parents are the greatest support system because they will not allow you to fail. Use their support and love to guide you. Confer with them freely and openly. Let them see and understand your goals and objectives so they can be free to give their support.

Friends: Friends are your lifeline to what the real world is about. They are your release from the pressures of being a student-athlete. Consider their advice wisely and always keep them in perspective of the whole picture.

Display your talents

Coaches will provide you with a scholarship if you can do one simple thing. That is, prove that you can compete at the collegiate level. Coaches want to see you display your talent. Always play against the best and toughest competition that you can. In lieu of them personally seeing you, they will accept the word of a recognized, and respected source; an assistant, scout, scouting service, alumnus or other respected source. Any one of the following means can be used to display your skill:

1) **Summer leagues**: Summer leagues in which many high schools compete, offer viewing opportunities of young pros-

pects. Also, competitive adult leagues and events represent opportunities for recognition.

2) **Camps and Schools**: Specialty schools and camps are amongst the most popular viewing opportunities for coaches. A lot of behind the scenes recruiting is done here.

3) **Pick-up Games**: They may not be a popular recruiting method, but these games can be very helpful in finding and locating pockets of talent. Pick-up games are the recruiting tools of peer recruiters. These "recruiters" may know someone who is in a position to make a decision or referral of your talent.

4) **Practice Sessions**: You may have heard the adage "practice like you are going to play." The way an athlete practices says a lot about an athletes potential, especially in individual sports. Always practice as if you are competing for the championship tomorrow.   Yes, coaches and scouts do attend practices too! A lot of times you will not even know that they are present.

5) **Regular Season Play**: The most popular opportunity to view athletic talent is against regular season opponents. However, regular season play, can represent a scouting dilemma for recruiters. First, they have to be sure that the competition, which the recruit faces, represents a credible challenge. Next, they always have concerns on the performance of the athlete. Is the performance demonstrated their personal best? Are they competing above their level because of a rivalry? Is it their best performance to date? Or, are they having a bad performance? Is this the worst performance of their lives? Nevertheless, if a coach or his staff is interested in your abilities and willing to make a scheduled appearance, you should expect more than one viewing.

6) **Game Film**: Game films may put the recruit in the driver's seat in the recruiting wars.   Similar to sending off a portfolio of your best work, is the impression that game film can make on a prospective coach. The game film (or tape) prepared should follow two rules of style: First, the film should be current, clear, and concise. If you are sending film, make sure the film represents a current regular season performance. The present makes a clear statement of your abilities, interest and consistency.

Second, make the recruiters job easy. Edit the film in such a way that you can be clearly distinguished from your teammates or competitors. It is always good to double check the film you are sending to ensure that you are easily distinguishable. In some cases it may even be helpful to use an editor which places a light colored highlight around you.

You might include a sheet with the tape which indicates your appearances and/or position. For instance, if your are the right fullback appearing at minutes 24-48, indicate so on the cheat sheet accompanying the film. This saves the recruiter time from wondering or mistaking your identity.

7) **Tournament Play**:   Probably the most compelling question about a student-athlete is his ability to perform at the next level.   That's why post-season play represents such a considerable statement of athletic performance. In addition, all records of your performance, film, and media weigh in your favor.

Sometimes the sport you play may not present you with the opportunities to participate in post-season or tournament play—with team sports it is certainly understandable. In those cases, your ranking or record against a post-season contender could be influential. Though influential, post-season play may not represent the end of the road where individual sports are involved. For instance, if you consistently compete against the number one ranked performer in your sport and offer competitive matches, that fact alone could be weighty in your favor. The bottom line is to use all methods of factual self-promotion at your disposal.

There are some great high school athletic programs with strong winning traditions, year after year, that produce college caliber athletes. Some such programs attract attention because the coach has a reputation for developing talent. Or, the coach has an eye for picking talented athletes who have not reached their full potential. Hopefully, you will at least compete against such a team during your high school career. The best position to be in as a prospective student athlete, is to have the recruiters initiate the interest. I wouldn't suggest transferring schools to follow an athletic dream, but remember to always compete against the best competition that you possibly can. Your breaks will always come with hard work!

8) **Reply to Your Inquiries**: Whether or not you are interested in a particular school, reply to every written inquiry that you receive. Always be thankful and grateful that you have had the opportunity to get the exposure. Intercollegiate athletics is a relatively close arena. Coaches come in contact with one another through, games, meetings and various activities on a fairly regular basis. No coaching job is permanent! The respect and courtesy you give tends to follow you.

9) **Initiate Inquiries**: There is nothing wrong with sending coaches a letter and resume expressing your interest in their school, and athletic program. Included with the letter should be some news clips, coaches recommendations, or evaluations, or other respectable third party opinion of your talent. Be sure to mention any awards, or honors you have received. Be warned! You may be unaware of the prescence of many recruiters who represent the programs of which you have an interest. Comptete your best in every practice and game you participate.

Chapter Six

The Healthy Athlete

The subject of health, as it relates to athletes, is the most critical of issues to a collegiate or pre-collegiate student-athlete. What goes in to the body and how the body is maintained has a direct affect on how the athlete will perform. By adhering to the basic rules regarding nutrition and injury prevention, you may find yourself exceeding even your own expectations.

Diet

For purposes of this section, the term diet, will refer both to caloric intake and the nutritional value. The goal of this section is to make you aware of some of the do's and don'ts of this aspect of training. We will not attempt to provide specific information, as that is beyond the scope of this guide. Fortunately there are many thorough references which provide specific training regimens and more detailed information regarding diet and nutrition. You will find some of those books in our Bibliography and Recommended Reading sections. We highly recommend that you pursue further reading on the subject.

For many years we have been inundated with information regarding diet and nutrition in the form of Recommended Dietary Allowances (RDAs). RDAs are not the standard by which athletes should adhere, for the following reasons: First, RDAs were never developed for athletes. Athletes were not the standard by which the recommendations were made, nor were the findings based upon studies of athletes. Accepting the results of the studies is the equivalent to applying lab results to humans based on the studies of rats. Secondly, no one diet fits all. Lifestyle (smoking, drinking), age, metabolism, air quality, training frequency, general health, medication, and many other factors are to be considered prior to constructing a specific diet. Lastly and most importantly, world renowned nutritionist, Dr. Michael Colgan sums it up best, in his book entitled Optimum Sports Nutrition, "If you use the RDAs to plan your nutrition, you will *never, never* reach your athletic potential.". Dr. Robert Haas, in his best selling book, Eat to Win, recommends a blood chemistry analysis for the active athlete. The purpose behind the analysis is to provide a detailed analysis of substances carried within the blood, how efficiently oxygen is used in the body, and other useful information.

Injury Prevention

Injury prevention is not an exact science, simply because there is no way to make an athlete injury proof. The goal behind injury prevention, is to make an athlete injury resistant. Injury resistance is achieved through proper and thorough preparation–mental as well as physical.

Injury Prevention should not be taken lightly. Young athletes are in the group most susceptible to injuries. Approximately "seventy percent of all sports injuries happen to athletes between the ages of ten and twenty-four." Almost forty percent of all injuries happen to children less than fifteen (Southmayd, 1981). Further, the more keen the competition, the greater the chance in receiving injury. Higher incidences of injury are reported at the collegiate level. Seventy-five percent of college athletes sustain injuries during any one year. Oddly enough studies indicate that the majority of injuries are sustained during practice. Many theories try to explain the tendency but none have proven absolutely conclusive. However, the following are some possible reasons why injuries occur:

1) **Improper warm-ups/cool downs**: Many athletes make the mistake of playing before a good warm-up and stretch before strenuous exercise. Prior to strenuous activity, the muscles should be warmed and stretched. To sustain and improve upon flexibility, it is recommended that at least five minutes should be dedicated to stretching before the end of the session.

2) **Poor conditioning**: Some athletes are under the assumption that getting back in to peak form will take little effort, so they tend to not exercise until two-a-day sessions (pre-season workouts) resume. Sadly the body doesn't work quite that way. As a general rule, the body needs to work at least three times as hard to get back in to condition as it does to maintain it.

3) **Sub-standard equipment or facilities**: Proper equipment, be it shoes, or head gear should always be in good condition. Appropriate medical staff and emergency equipment should be available at practices as well as at games.

4) **Overuse**: Sometimes the body needs rest after being

pushed to its limit. Healing and strengthening occurs during rest. Without proper rest, the body becomes more susceptible to injury.

5) **Poor diet**: Athletes need to eat well planned, nutritional meals. Food not only provides energy, but it also heals.

6) **Exceeding Limitations**: As athletes, we have heard of many stories of athletes that play with injuries. In fact, odds are strong that the average athlete, will compete injured in at least one sporting event in his career. However no one should play *hurt*. Playing hurt is to exceed the limitations the body has established for proper healing. For example, to continue in an event with a broken bone or pulled muscle until the point of exhaustion or breakdown may cause long-term damage. Many athletes fail to "listen" to their body. If an activity requires you to participate while enduring pain, then, you are probably in need of medical attention. Always listen to your body. Pain is an excellent indicator that something is wrong.

Before beginning any program, you should know your limitations. An examination by a qualified sports medicine physician should be your first step in preventing injuries (Kibler, 1990). The exam is a comprehensive look at the athlete's health. A physician or sports clinic near you can be contacted for further information or through:

> The American College of Sports Medicine
> 401 West Michigan Street
> Indianapolis, IN 46202-3233

Chapter Seven

Tips, Techniques, and Secrets

Stay motivated about your opportunities for success! Maintain a positive mental attitude and be enthusiastic about yourself. If you are enthusiastic about your abilities, that enthusiasm will carry over to the coach or recruiter. Maintain complete and absolute belief in your abilities.

Eclecticism

No this is not some new religion. To be *eclectic* is to select the best among many possible options. Improve always! There is always some area in which you can improve yourself. You can always be faster, stronger, smarter, more accurate, etc., etc., The minute you think that there is no room for improvement, is the minute that you have settled for mediocrity. True success can only happen through adopting this philosophy.

Time management

Time management is the management of time, and more. It is a skill that involves setting priorities, scheduling, and commitment. When you compete at the collegiate level, you will realize how valuable this skill. You will be pulled in various directions. You will have to prioritize your life–who you see and how long you see them. Get in the habit now. Take the process day by day and set a schedule to which you feel comfortable.

Time is your most valuable resource. Do not waste it! Schedule wisely. Monitor your study time, your social life, your work outs, the correspondence you send, and other activities that impact your day. After a month or two evaluate your progress and time management skills. Are you meeting your goals? Is your life easier? If you can say yes to those two questions, then you have a manageable schedule.

Consistency

Consistency is the most important athletic characteristic to have. It is important to be "consistently, consistent." That is, maintain balance in all that you pursue. Strive to do as well in class as you do in sports. Always practice and play your best. Each performance should demonstrate your level of skill and ability at the collegiate level. Do not let substandard performers bring you down to their level. Always dictate to your teammates, and competition, the level at which you practice and play.

Publicity

Publicity is so easy to generate, especially if you are consistent. Publicity comes in the form of respect from your teammates, coaches, peers, educators, friends and family. Consistent performance breeds consistent results. Pretty soon you generate your own publicity through the records you set, the all-star teams of which you are a member, and the dedication you have to being a well-rounded individual.

Publicity (news clips, scouting reports, etc.) may sometime have a negative impact. Use your reports sparingly, maybe if you are mentioned because of a record breaking or post-season performance. Few coaches like to be flooded with *local* news clips. Publicity also comes in the form of video tapes, and letters from coaches as well. As you have guessed by now, your publicity begins with your *reputation*. Maintain the reputation of a hard worker, and a consistent performer and your breaks will come.

Tangibles

The *tangibles* are the visible statistics, results, characteristics, and performances of a student-athlete. They appear in the box scores in the newspapers and scouting reports.

The personal statistics include your physical characteristics, personal abilities, and athletic accomplishments to date. Intangibles are the elements of your performance that does not appear in the box scores or stat sheets. Make sure that you promote your ability to lead and work hard, as well as you do your personal statistics.

Competition

Compete against other athletes so that you can improve your skills, and study from the experience. From almost every competition, you should put yourself in a position that enables you to improve your ranking and overall performance. Study the areas in which weakness has been exposed and improve on that area.

Camps

Our reference section lists directories available for your purchase, of athletic camps and schools across the nation. Among other things, look for the camps and schools which provide multiple levels of skill development (beginning, intermediate, advanced), experienced staff, written individual player reviews and assessments, and quality facilities.

Physical Health

Maintain total body fitness at all times. To do this requires constant dedication to your diet, maintaining physical and mental conditioning.

Preparation

Before any competition always do your own homework. We have a tendency to rely on what the scouts say or what the papers say about a team or individual without actually "seeing" for ourselves.   Always enter a competition physically and mentally prepared so that you can deal with almost any type of situation that arises.

Visualization

Visualize your success! Be enthusiastic about what you see at the end of your tunnel. Visualize your personal success story of receiving offers and eventually a full athletic scholarship.

Never give up on your dream. Always believe in your ability to succeed. With every little success, visualize how it will fit into the whole picture.

Training Tips

In this section we focus on two training circumstances, one, of which you may encounter during your athletic career. These circumstances involve your physical preparation for an event or team (see also Walk-ons page 78).

Post-season and pre-season conditioning is an important aspect of being a collegiate athlete. For instance, coaches like to make sure that the players are lifting, running, or in some way exercising or "thinking" about their sport during the regular academic year. Pre-season or off-season workouts focus on improving conditioning and sharpening skills.

Your preparation for the collegiate athletic career is a little different. Your preparation is totally centered around *time*. If you are a pre-high school athlete, you are in a most admirable position because you have the most time to develop all-around. If you are a high school student-athlete, depending on your age, you will use a more long range development strategy (beyond one year). If you are a senior or walk-on prospect, then you will probably focus on the short-term strategies.

A Short -term Program

Although your overall goal is to receive a full athletic scholarship, you should understand that the short-term program is the toughest. The odds of receiving a full-scholarship are against you, but, it is not impossible. First, and foremost, know and understand the rules to which you will be affected. Among the many qualifying factors for athletic eligibility, are admission and age. In all cases, you must be enrolled at the school in which you wish participate. Check with the ruling or legislative department of the association over which your prospective school is regulated, *before* you try-out, as the rules are always being updated.

Secondly, as a walk-on prospect it is important that you make written and verbal contact with the head coach prior to your participating in any athletic activity. By initiating contact in writing, you are putting your credentials on record. If you have documentation of your performance(s) available, i.e. newspaper clippings, video tape, film, indicate so in the letter. Use a follow-up call as a means of verifying that the head coach has received the letter and that you have the materials available for his review.

Thirdly, know what the practice and try-out schedule is for your sport. For some sports, the practice/try-out sessions may begin before the first day of classes allowing you the opportunity to be seen before registering for classes. Be informed that this option varies from sport to sport. Some sports do not begin their practice sessions until the school term has begun. In these cases, you would have to enroll in classes and pay for tuition for that particular semester.

Fourth, spread your options. Apply to more than one school and make contact with more than one coach.

Fifth, make sure that all your paperwork is in order. You should have an unofficial copy of your transcripts, and a physical.

Sixth, make sure that you are in the best shape of your life! If you are in better shape than your competitors or returning athletes, all the better. You want to impress the coach with your physical attributes–strength, power, endurance, stamina, flexibility, speed, quickness, and agility.

Make sure your skills, especially the basic skills, are well developed (for purposes of this example, we assume that you are attempting to try-out for an athletic system in which you believe you fit). You should be able to demonstrate a skill level comparable to the competition the program faces. Your scouting results should indicate to you the area in which your prospective team needs, help. Your advantage is knowing this information, and then demonstrating through performance at practice, that you are the answer. You should have an eye-catching skill or ability that the coach realizes his program can not do without.

With less than three months to train, it is important that skill and athletic ability is at an optimal. In addition to training, it is important that you compete as well. At least one day a week you should compete and do nothing else. If you are not in a situation where you are on a formal team (for such sports as track or golf), make a practice session your "game day." If you play a team sport, such as hockey, lacrosse, or football, it is pretty tough sometimes, to get a realistic, pick-up game. Compete against your training partner(s) to create the most realistic "game-day", conditions possible. Your realistic conditions should include using the mandatory equipment.

Set-up a Twelve week training program consisting of two phases, an eight week phase and a four week phase. For the first eight weeks, your emphasis is on improving your skills, enhancing your athletic attributes, and competing in game-like conditions. Train at least once a day, five days a week. You determine the duration, based on your understanding of your ability and the level of ability at the prospective program.

During the four week phase, train at least twice a day, five days a week for the first three weeks prior to the try-outs. During the last week train only to maintain the skills and abilities you have been developing for the last eleven weeks. Train every other day with the first practice in the last week being the most strenuous. Stretch every day during the week and work out any tightness or "kinks." These tips may also be applied if you are attempting to make high school varsity.

Mid-term program (3 months to a year)

If you are preparing to walk-on to a program, it is important (given this time frame) that you participate in the most competitive and organized league that you can. Doing so, leaves a much better impression than not being involved in something organized. To some, organization means discipline. In cases where organized play is not possible, document your training routine, and stick to it religiously. If necessary, go back to your high school and compete at practice sessions (if possible). If you compete for at least three months or so, in the course of a year, you may want to follow our suggestions regarding a three month program.

Academic Tips

We've seen it and heard it many times...athlete ruled ineligible due to academic deficiency. A majority of the time, the deficiencies are due to none other than poor training and preparation. Half the challenge in receiving an athletic scholarship offer is proving yourself academically capable to handle a college curriculum. For the athlete who may not know what to expect from college academically, here are a few helpful tips.

College Life vs. High School

The most important aspect of succeeding academically as a student-athlete is time management. Get in the habit of planning your classes, study time, practice time, extracurricular, and private time on at least a weekly basis. A college curriculum and high school curriculum are different. In high school, you are given a body of information to remember and you are required to demonstrate your knowledge of the information through tests or presentations. Many courses are geared to provide information (such as a history course) without that information necessarily having a direct impact on subsequent courses. The focal point of the courses is to provide general information and to give the student a foundation on which he can develop his thoughts. Most college level courses impart *building block* information. For example, information learned in a second lecture, or course, will assume an understanding of the subject from the first lecture or course. And so on with subsequent lectures and courses. In addition, the information learned at a level one statistics class will have a definite impact on upper level psychology or business courses. Everything is interrelated. However most students will not realize the correlation of information and ideas until they begin to take their upper level courses. When you hear of a high school (or a high school student) that maintains a college preparatory curriculum the reference is to both the intensity and depth of the curriculum and the method in which it is presented to students. A college level curriculum will include at least the following:

> Four years of English
> Three years of Math
> Two years of Foreign Language
> Two years of History
> Three years of Science
> Two years of Liberal Arts

For the extra edge you may want to include as your electives, a typing course and several computer courses. Check with your high school guidance counselor for recommendations and your perspective colleges as to their academic entrance requirements.

GPA Determines Your Entrance Into College

Many student-athletes are under the mistaken impression that their grades and grade point average (GPA) will not affect their scholarship opportunities if they are very talented athletes. This thinking couldn't be further from the truth, because grades and grade point average will definitely affect the number and quality of offers a student-athlete can expect to receive. In addition, grades and grade point averages become a very important factor for athletes wishing to concentrate in a certain field of study. Some colleges (within a university system) will refuse to accept an athlete into the college if the grades are not up to par.

All institutions which conform to NAIA, NCAA and NJCAA standards are required to abide by the academic standards set for the general student population. This means that a specific grade point average will have to be maintained as well as a full-time course load in order to maintain *academic* eligibility. In almost all cases, failure to maintain academic eligibility is grounds to discontinue the scholarship arrangement the institution has with the student-athlete. To avoid any possible academic problems, follow our guidelines for academic success.

Academic Success Guidelines

Success traits

It's been said that, "in order to be successful, one has to do what successful people do." No one is born smart. Smart people do little things that make them successful. Here are just a few tips:

A place to study

Many schools now require that their freshmen athletes attend mandatory study halls. The purpose of the study hall is to provide an environment for learning. Many freshmen athletes will find themselves succumbing to distractions, or in need of resources (i.e. tutoring), outside the normal environment. Study halls provide the academic resources under properly supervised conditions to which a young student may not be accustomed. After a certain time, the athlete may want to select his own time and place to study. At which time, the library is highly recommended.

Time management

Part of your organization plan must include time management. The reason that time management is so critical is because it (time) is easily taken for granted. As an athlete you may have extra demands placed upon your time, not allowing you to accomplish what you expect. Many events will occur at the same time, such as exams, placing additional demands on time. In general, the better you plan your time, the more effective you will be as a student-athlete. Time management requires planning and execution. Simply monitor your daily, weekly, and monthly events from sunup to sunrise. Monitor those tasks which you have completed, are in progress, and those which need to be completed in the future. It is essential, to your execution, that you set deadlines and adhere closely to them.

Work in groups

Where possible work in groups. For example studying for an exam with a classmate is often more effective than studying by yourself. Discussion and questions are frequently raised and there is a strong tendency for one to help the other. Of course, select a study partner who is at least equal to your abilities and ambition.

Study time

As a student-athlete, *time*, is your most important asset. Study time is no exception. The average class schedule (12-15 credit hours per semester) will require you to spend about three to four hours a night in quiet study. In addition, weekly reviews of material covered during prior periods will help you to grasp the material.

Avoid procrastinating work

The most common mistake many students make concerning school is *procrastinating.* Pushing school work off to the side until the last possible minute just creates needless anxiety. In addition, retention of the course material is reduced, which can lead to problems in related courses. The key to staying on top of your school work is organization. Set up a routine, using your time management schedule as your guide. No one could be expected to adhere to a daily routine 100 % of the time, but less than 90% of the time will eventually lead to trouble. "Plan your work, and work your plan."

Be prepared for class

Be prepared for each class from the first day through the end of the period. Preparation includes, doing the required home-work and asking any questions in areas in which you did not understand. Preparation also involves reading or studying ahead of time, allowing the lecture to reinforce or expound upon the material you have pre-viewed.

Excellent attendance

Attending class on a regular basis is very difficult for a student-athlete. Traveling and other schedule conflicts will normally not allow perfect attendance. However, many in-structors teach more than one class, so attending the same lecture on a different day may keep you at par with the other students.

Besides your physical presence, it is very important to be mentally present during class time as well. Staying up to the wee hours will only limit how effective you will be as a student.

Homework

Above all else, turn in your assignments on or before the due date. Many instructors deduct points off the assignment grade or the final grade of students that routinely turn in their assignments late. Conversely, you may be able to gain the instructors favor by regularly turning your assignments in early.

Understand all instructions, lectures, and assignments

Do not be afraid or embarrassed to ask questions. Odds are, at least one other person has the same question you do. Ask a questions if you do not understand a lecture, assignment, or instructions. Never be too proud to ask for help if you need it.

Complete projects in phases

Complete your long projects and assignments in phases. Doing so will allow for proper feedback from your instructor or experts on the subject. Set deadlines for the completion of each phase and try to stick to them. For example, if you have a research project that is a semester-long project separate the major tasks. Task one might be to collect preliminary research so that you can develop an outline. You may find it necessary to make telephone calls to collect information or to arrange for interviews. Part two might involve approaching your instructor with your outline so that you may refine your subject. Next, you would develop a rough draft. Lastly, you would prepare your final drafts and practice your presentation.

Prioritize

As we have stated before, *organization* is the key to success. Your organization includes time management. Time management involves prioritizing so that the most important needs get taken care of first and on time. Time management also involves managing your practice, study, and social time. In fact, any event that can potentially take critical time away from or add to your day should be planned.

Review regularly

A skill critical to learning is memory. Memory can only occur if familiarity exists. For many of us, true recall (a form of memory that allows us to retrieve facts, dates, names, events, etc.) mostly occurs through repetition. Take time, maybe two or three hours each Saturday reviewing notes, lectures, and required reading so that you become familiar with the subject. An individual who can *recall* facts, be it formulas, quotes, or theories is a student in control of their academic success.

Teach yourself as much as possible

Teach yourself as much about the subject as possible. Gathering information in addition to what is required of you in class will widen your perspective and put into focus the concepts which may be unclear.

Take good notes

Being able to write clear and accurate notes is an important and valuable skill. It is also a skill that you will be regularly using throughout your college career. There are many methods to good note taking. Any good book on the subject will provide you with several alternatives. Perhaps you may even develop your own system.

Understand the academic structure

How will you be graded? How much does class participation count toward your final grade? What do you need to do to get an A or B grade from the instructor? Where do you need to go to get your report typed? How intense is the class? Will you get four hours of homework each night from the instructor? Is it recommended that you take a certain class in the off-season? Know the answer to these and other questions which will affect the final grade.

Improve on rudimentary skills if required

Be prepared to do college level work. You should be well adept at reading, writing, and math prior to taking your tougher classes. As always, if you are not proficient in an area, seek help.

Know the requirements of your major

Some of the greatest errors made concerning academics center around class selection. Many student-athletes find out at the end of an academic year, or worse, before graduation, that they will need to take an additional class or two (during the summer). Some athletes are shocked to learn that many schools don't pay for athlete's summer classes. These same athletes are again shocked to learn that they may not graduate. Or worse, these athletes lose their scholarship because of athletic ineligibility.

To avert any problems, make sure the classes you are taking are approved by the appropriate college advisors. If you are a transfer student, make sure you have your transcript(s) reviewed so that you get the proper credit for the classes you have taken.

Use the syllabus

Most instructors try to be very accommodating with answering questions and helping students succeed in their course. Many provide tools, such as a *syllabus*, to help students succeed. The syllabus is an outline of the lectures, assignments, grading system, exam schedules, and other pertinent information made available to the student (normally provided in the first or second class). Use the syllabus to assist you in your time management.

Setting

Setting plays a vital role in being a successful student-athlete. For serious student-athletes living in an on-campus dorm is an open invitation for distractions. Traveling can also upset the normal study routine. However, it is important to find your special place where you know you can study in a quiet, uninterrupted area. The best place to start is always the library.

Pick up the extra points

When possible, always pick up the extra points for class participation, attendance, or homework assignments. Many times those points can make the difference from being a high B or a low A.

Walking-on

When your an unknown, be it at the high school, college, or professional level, the odds are stacked against your making the team. Here a few tips which increase your chances for success.

Be Punctual: One of the best ways to make a good impression is to arrive at a try-out thirty minutes early. Never be late! Arriving late gives an impression that the team is not important. This is the last impression that you want to give to a coach.

Physically fit: I've attended a lot of try-outs in my lifetime and I can say without a doubt that the level of physical condition plays an important part in determining a final selection. When you appear at a try-out be in excellent physical condition.

Skill level: Be confident in your skills and be free to demonstrate them when appropriate. By demonstration, we mean to display your mastery of the fundamentals in such a manner that indicates your skill level. The trick is to be relaxed and poised , and to portray your confidence to coaches that are watching. It's important to take advantage of the opportunities to display skills—do not "hot-dog." Being a hot-dog will only turn a coach off.

Sport Knowledge: There is nothing more refreshing for a coach than to have a leader that understands the subtleties of the sport on his team. Knowledge is gained through playing, observing, and studying your sport.

Display teamwork: Of course, if you are a tennis player you do not have to worry about this too much, do you? Quite the contrary. College tennis is as much a team sport as an individual sport. Your teammates need support at practice and games just as much as a basketball player needs it. Teamwork is something that can extend beyond the playing field.

Have an eye-catching gimmick: Whether you possess great speed, size, skills, or quickness, you must be able to contribute in a purely unique manner. Every athlete possesses a quality that is purely unique. The athlete that is able to demonstrate the need for his gifts is the athlete who makes the team or gets the scholarship.

Extra Income Techniques

As a general rule, restrictions are imposed on institutions which provide athletic scholarships.   However, most of the college students I know need some spending money for dating, laundry, or toiletries.   There are a few instances where your athletic scholarship can present you with opportunities for spending money. As are rule, student-athletes are not compensated to participate in their sports activities. However, compensation by way of stipend is a recognized procedure allowable under certain circumstances. Your institution and governing association may determine if you would be eligible to receive the funds.   Once aid (your scholarship) is granted, it is yours as long as you maintain your eligibility.

If you receive a room allotment on your grant-in-aid, your rent has been ruled to have a monetary value. You could request a stipend if you room off-campus. Your goal, in such a case, would be to maintain the   same dollar value in rent but decrease your expenses. For instance, if your monthly allotment comes to $500 you may want to room share with a teammate with an equal allotment. At the beginning of every month, together (your roommate and yourself) you receive $1000 for rent. Pay the rent off (i.e. rent of $500) and split the difference between yourselves. Of course, you may have to make a deposit for the rent.

The second method of receiving spending money also involves the "room" item on the grant-in-aid.   At some institutions you may find a housing referral list or department which coordinates students with available off-campus housing. You may even find a situation in which you may be able to receive housing in exchange for performing a service. In exchange for monthly rent maybe you could perform some household services for a family. In this case, let's say that your room award is $2,700 per academic year (nine months). Monthly, you would receive a stipend check for $300

($2,700/9). That is three hundred dollars per month, in additional spending money.

Teach your Sport

Another possible way of earning money in your sport while a student-athlete, is to instruct youngsters during summer camp. There are specific rules that specify how student-athletes are to be employed as counselors. Most ruling associations mandate that the money you earn from work must not exceed a full scholarship amount (although this rule applies during the regular school year). Be sure to check with your school's head coach, athletic director, or the association to which your school is a a member before making any such arrangements (as it may jeopardize your eligibility).

Managing and Playing Two or More Sports

In earlier chapters we discussed the importance of maintaining balance. We also mentioned the importance of having a variety of skills and abilities. The greater the variety, generally the greater the opportunities you will have for an athletic scholarship. Take that philosophy even further and participate in two sports in high school.

At first, playing two sports may seem like it would be burdensome. Not so, if the two sports complement each other. For instance, If you play tennis, you might want to consider baseball. Both sports complement each other in that each requires a high degree of hand-to-eye coordination. If your sport is soccer, participating in track or cross country would complement the running that is done in soccer. Basketball players should consider volleyball or high jumping on the track team to complement the reaction and jumping skills.

Some recruiters will look more favorably to a dual sport athlete, especially if the second sport involves developing or maintaining a set of vital skills. Sports for which objective figures are provided, (i.e. track and field) do nothing but heighten a prospects chances of receiving a full athletic scholarship.

Development

Participating in two sports and performing well is a challenging yet reachable feat. The most important aspect about learning anything is to establish the fundamental knowledge or skills. Once the fundamental skills are developed, you can be rest assured that any lapse or time off will do little to deteriorate the skill level. As always skill development comes over time with formal practice and competition. Learning advanced skills is most often developed through extra instruction, for instance through, sports camps. You will find that it will take longer for the body to master a new set of sport skills than it will take to respond to conditioning. Long story short, if you want to try to learn a new sport, begin by mastering the fundamental skills of the game first. Develop the athletic skills second.

Maintenance of skills and conditioning.

Each sport adheres to it's own set of conditioning regimen. If you want to enhance your abilities and college prospects, it is generally better to participate in dual sports which complement one another over those that supplement one another. For example, sports which complement one another are basketball and volleyball. Basketball complements volleyball because it (basketball) requires a tremendous amount of running as well as jumping and quickness. Volleyball complements basketball through its (volleyball's) demands for quick reactions and timing. Sports which supplement one another, such as soccer and baseball, tend to keep one active without greatly enhancing skills or directly improving athletic ability in either sport. While stamina and endurance is important in soccer, it is not so important in baseball. Conversely, the running done in baseball could hardly impact the conditioning required in soccer. These two sports are all together different. After all, how often are you allowed to use your hands in soccer?

Even when sports are complementary, a certain amount of skill deterioration is bound to occur. However, once the fundamental skills have been mastered, a relatively short amount of time is needed to retrieve the skills. A good way to maintain the skill levels of sports is to periodically return to them –just to compete for fun! This way, you allow your body to "refresh" itself of the skills in a relaxed environment. For example, if you play baseball and tennis, and are in the middle of tennis season, play a little catch or softball in your spare time. By doing so, you use a similar set of skills, although you apply them differently.

In cases where participation in one sport, supplements the other, it is important to begin a program of maintenance. The goal is to make sure that skill and athletic deterioration is kept to a minimum. Such is the case, between golf and track. In our example, golf, a sport requiring intense concentration, and comparatively little physical exertion could not offer the physical challenges of track. In such cases, it is important to develop a routine that allows for simple maintenance over all else. The goal, during golf season, would be to maintain a routine that would allow you to run for times which are a challenge, but not over exerting. For instance, if you are a quarter-miler whose best time is 52 seconds, train two or three times a week to reach times of 70 or 75 seconds. It is about three to four times more difficult to get back in to physical shape as it is to maintain it.

Creating and enriching opportunities

We believe that participation in more than one sport can do nothing but improve your opportunities for a scholarship. Certainly, excelling academically and participating in two or more sports will generate all the publicity you could ever want.

Other scholarship opportunities

There are scholarship opportunities outside the playing field itself which are available at many institutions. In most cases, they are not full-scholarships but they may supplement your aid. A position, such as team manager, may avail you of some of the opportunities of being an athlete. Essentially, the duty of team manager is to make sure that the minor details are handled. For instance, the team manager would be responsible for making sure that the uniforms are cleaned and prepared. Sometimes the Team Manager may assist in compiling team statistics, coordinating or maintaining team supplies, and making sure that the water is in the cooler. If your major is related to medicine or sports medicine there may be an opportunity for you within the athletic department staff. The department may pay you, outright, for your services. Or you may receive some form of assistance from the department. Team statisticians positions are available sometimes, if the department can afford them. As the position suggests, the statistician's job is to record and analyze statistics which help the coaching staff make decisions.

Appendix
and
Other Back Matter

Appendix

Training Routines

Although not a requirement, we strongly recommend, before proceeding with any of the physical training programs in the book, that you have a physical examination. You should be diagnosed as physically fit, and well enough to perform the strenuous exercise programs described. In addition we advise that an evaluation of your muscle and bone strength be conducted.

In previous sections I mentioned that certain physical abilities can be enhanced and we will show you how. Our emphasis with these drills is to make you, stronger, more powerful, quicker, more agile, and increase your endurance and stamina. As we go through the exercises we will explain the theory behind them so that you understand the benefit of doing them correctly. Before you begin the programs, document any times, distances, reps, or other measures of your ability so that, weeks later, you can compare the results. For best results, do the following drills in the order presented: 1) bounding, 2) step-ups, 3) half squats, and 4) calf raises.

Lower Body Training (Bounding Drills)

Our first drills involve a technique know as bounding (also know as plyometrics). The techniques originated from the former U.S.S.R. and were part of a total exercise regimen. Many track athletes may be familiar with some of the offshoots of the exercises. Before beginning the routine, you should be thoroughly stretched and warmed-up. DO NOT attempt to do bounding if you are cold—severe muscle damage, including muscle pulls can occur (we suggest a 10-15 minutes of light running or cycling on a stationary bicycle as a warm-up). Always stretch, prior to the exercises.   NEVER use weight resistance equipment (especially ankle weights) with the bounding regimen as you will damage your ankles or leg bones. If you have a regular practice routine, we suggest that you conduct the bounding exercises BEFORE regular practice so that your maximum strength is utilized. The step-ups, half squats, and calf raises can be done after practice. This exercise requires an advanced level of stamina and endurance when being performed. You should be on a regular exercise regimen before attempting the program.

Our first power exercise requires that you find yourself a fairly well cushioned but firm surface, such as a wood floor, rubberized surface or grassy field (never perform on concrete). The area you will need does not have to be large (on average, a space four feet by four feet). The clearance space over your head should be at least five feet. If using an athletic field, make sure that it is not saturated with water (the benefit of the exercise would be fairly minimal). Your goal throughout the exercise is to jump or bound as high as possible, a minimum of 20-35 consecutive times. These bounds are called two-legged power bounds because you are jumping straight up utilizing (equally) the power in both legs. With each jump, you are trying to reach the sky. When you come down to earth, DO NOT RECOIL! Jump as high as you can again, as soon as you touch the ground

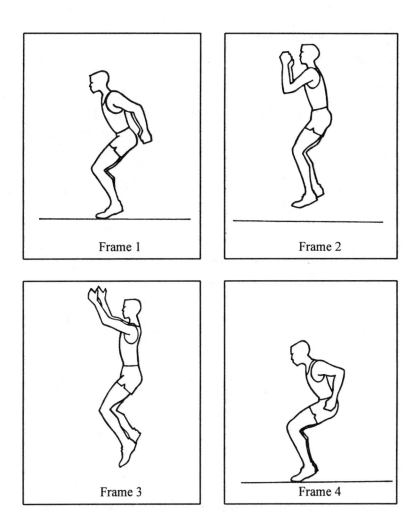

Frame 1

Frame 2

Frame 3

Frame 4

(see frames 1-4).   Use your arms to give yourself added momentum—swing them up and through to the sky! Prepare to land and jump again. Once you finish the first set, rest. Your rest should be long enough that you have energy to do another complete set, but short enough that your muscles do not get cold (approx. 60-90 seconds). You should not exceed 3 sets of 35 bounds per day. We do not recommend the sets be performed more than five days per week. If you are on a weight training program, do the bounding before you go to a strenuous lower body workout. Make sure that you do the bounding only on the days that you do your weight training or else your muscles will burn-out.

How the technique works (an overview): Bounding is effective because you are "programming" your muscles to perform in a certain manner. Specifically you are programming your muscles to move and react powerfully. The muscles you are programming are the calf muscles of the lower leg, the quadriceps, hamstrings, and gluteus muscles. You will notice in a short time that several things will happen as a result of your bounding. You will very shortly notice increases in acceleration, vertical leap, speed, and quickness. Though the results may vary with each individual, you should begin realizing considerable gains in as little as four weeks.

Our next performance drill is usually used in combination with the bounding drill to add to your level of performance. This drill is a step-up drill. The purpose of this drill is to isolate the hamstring and gluteus muscles—the key muscles for increasing speed, vertical, leap, and quickness. You begin by positioning your right foot on a box, chair, or some other solid object which allows an eighty to ninety degree bend at the knee. The object must, continuously, be able to support your body weight. If you begin the exercise with your left foot, your right foot should be flat on the ground allowing the leg to be almost straight. Using and concentrating only on the left leg, use a quick burst of power to raise your body off the ground to a position which allows both feet to be side by side on the top of the box. To descend, keep the right foot on the box and let the left leg come to the ground (see frames 5 & 6). The motion is a stair climbing motion. It is similar to the motion you would use except for the fact that you are not ascending stairs. Each time both legs do one ascending motion it is a repetition. Your aim is to do a minimum of one set of one hundred repetitions per day. To get the full benefit of the exercise you must be

Frame 5

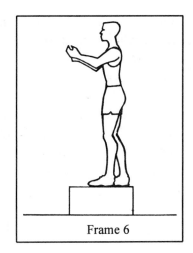

Frame 6

certain that the foot on the box or step is used, exclusively, to help raise your entire body. There should be no assistance from the leg that is straight or from the hands and arms being used for balance. You should be exploding with power with every burst. Tip: When doing the exercise your knee should not be in a position to go beyond the vertical plain of your foot (see frame 7). To do so may cause pain in the knee joints (Lindsey, 1983). In addition, the bend at the knee should be as close to 90° as possible (frame 5). A greater angle will not be of benefit (see frame 8). A lessor angle may cause injury or pain (see frame 7). If you have a history of tendonitis you may find some discomfort when conducting this exercise. Quad raises and leg extensions should lesson the discomfort, as they have the result of strengthening the muscles in front of the leg and over the knee. Done correctly, you will definitely see gains within four weeks.

Lastly, strength exercises for the quads, and calf, muscles should be done. For quad power do only half squats (see frame 9). These are regular leg squats, with the exception that you bend down to an angle, forty-five to sixty degrees at the knee, rather than a ninety degree angle. Again the purpose is to "program" your legs to act and respond for power, speed, and quickness. You bend down no farther than a forty-five degree angle (when you run or jump your knees do not bend at an angle larger than forty-five degrees upon impact with a surface). Did you bend your knee at a ninety degree angle to jump as high as you could, or was it closer to forty-five degrees? Your goal for this exercise is to do no less than half the number of repetitions you did for the step-ups. You may use a small amount of weight such as ten or twenty pounds of weight held in your hands or on

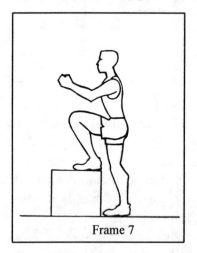

Frame 7

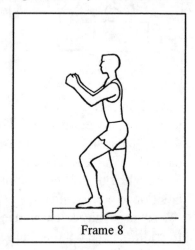

Frame 8

your shoulders. Be wary that you do not overmatch the strength in your hamstrings. To do so, will make your hamstrings vulnerable to muscle pulls. Tip: The source of power is in the movement upward. For example, as I perform one repitition of a squat, I make sure to move smoothly and slowly from the standing position, downward to an angle that is between forty-five and ninety

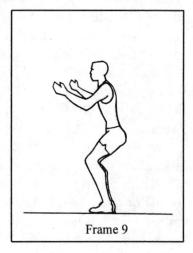

Frame 9

degrees. To complete the rep, my movement upward is smooth and quick, making sure NOT to lock my knees at the end of the movement.

Your calf muscle exercises (calf raises) are to be performed one leg at a time. Position yourself on a surface at least four inches in height to allow for a full range of motion in the lower leg area (the bottom stair on a staircase should suffice as it will accommodate a full range of motion as well as help to balance you). The balls of your feet should be on the surface, your heels should be overhanging the edge. You may use as much weight as your muscles will allow, however if you do calf raises daily, your body weight is sufficient. Exercise one leg at a time. Conduct the exercise with the toes pointed in three different directions. The first position is toes pointed straight forward. The second positioned is toes pointed at an angle forty-five degrees inward. The third and final position is toes pointed at an angle forty-five outward. One full motion down and up is one repetition. Complete at least one set in each direction (straight, forty-five degrees inward, and forty-five degrees outward) with each leg daily.

Upper Body Strength Training (Calisthenics)

Gaining strength can be achieved using many different methods. Our primary method of strength training is calisthenics (exercises performed, mostly, without the benefit of some type of apparatus). These exercises are push-ups, pull-ups, sit-ups, and dips.

Push-ups: The first style of push-ups requires that your hands be positioned just outside each shoulder as you begin in the down position (you are face down, your torso is touching the ground, your knees are straight, and the balls of your feet are on the ground). While keeping your upper body rigid and your knees straight, use your arms to raise your body until your arms are straight (this is the up position). Lower your body to the down position to complete one repetition. To work more chest (pectoral muscles) widen the position of your hands when you are in the down position. To work more of the back of the arm (the triceps), bring the hands closer to the middle of the chest (the closer the hands, the more the triceps will work). Tip: If you can not do a pull-up yet, do three sets (one set of each style) of push-ups, three times a week. You should begin at a pace where you are able to perform an equal number of reps at each set. For example, if you are able to perform 20 regular, 15 pectoral, and 15 tricep push-ups, start your next session doing one set of 20 reps of each style. Once your are able to go through two sessions, without failure, add 3-5 reps to each set.

Pull-ups: A pull-up bar is at the appropriate height, if, as you hang from the bar, your legs are straight and your feet do not touch the ground. Enough clearance should exist so that your chin can be safely raised over the bar in the "up" position. To begin, hang from a bar (palms facing you or palms facing away from you) hands shoulder width apart. Next, pull yourself straight up until your chin is just over the bar. Lower yourself down to the starting position to complete one repetition. Tip: We recommend that advanced athletes perform pull-ups, palms facing away. Beginners should perform pull-ups, palms facing inward (they are much easier). To work more shoulders spread the hands apart. To work more arms, bring the hands closer together. If you are doing three sets of push-ups, you should begin your pull-up routine with one-fourth to one-half the amount of push-ups. Using fifteen push-ups as our guide, 5 pull-ups should be your initial goal. Increase the intensity by adding a second set. Advance one to two pull-ups each set, if you are able to complete two sessions without fail. For those of you who are unable to do pull-ups, build up to them by doing the three basic styles of push-ups mentioned in the push-up section.

Dips: Dips are an exercise for the back of the arms (triceps) and shoulders. To perform this exercise you will need a chair or a parallel bar type of apparatus which will tolerate a 90° bend at the elbow. Ideally, your starting position will be arms straight and body elevated. If this position is not possible, be sure that the downward motion (the motion creating the bend in the elbow) extends beyond 90° so a full range of motion is possible. To begin, lower your entire body until there is at least 90° bend at the elbow. Raise yourself to the starting position to complete one repetition. Tip: Do dips after doing pull-ups and push-ups. Dips are easier to perform after pull-ups and push-ups are done.

Sit-ups: The most important exercise an athlete can perform. Sit-ups are your key to speed and power. Many variations prevail, but I believe the more effective ones are done flat on the floor. To begin, you should lie flat, with your back on the floor. Clasp your hands lightly behind your head. Bend your knees and bring your legs off the ground. Your upper legs should be perpendicular to the ground and your lower legs should be parallel to the ground (your lower body will form an "L" shape). For the first repetition, raise your right shoulder off the ground, allowing your elbow to touch your left knee which should be moving towards your chest. Lower your right shoulder and your left knee. Next, do the same movement, but raise your left shoulder and allow the right knee to meet the left elbow. You have just completed one repetition. Your goal is to perform one hundred per day (five days per week).

Testing the Results

A true measure of strength is measured by one's ability to manipulate his or her body weight. Most strength tests are administered using some type of apparatus (we test on free weights). As a general rule, we recommend using the bench press to measure upper body strength. A good score would be one in which you test at 1.0 (100% of your body). For example, if your are 200 hundred pounds then, minimally you should be able to bench press 200 pounds two times. Some sports, such as football may demand that your ratio be higher, i.e. 1.5. (200 pounds x 1.5 = 300 pounds). A good lower body test, would be 2.0. Again, using our model two hundred pound athlete as our model, a good squat test would be four hundred pounds lifted two times.

A word of caution: If you perform the squat test, be sure to perform the leg curl test as well (A good score is 1.6—eighty percent of squat maximum). If a significant disparity of strength between the quadriceps (the major upper-leg muscles in front of the thigh) and the hamstrings (the major upper-leg muscles behind the thigh) exists, the possibility of a severe muscle pull or tear is great. These three tests are the most basic measures of strength. They should not be performed by preadolescent youth, nor should the testing be administered without first counseling a professional . These basic tests are not designed to detect weak muscles. They are designed to determine muscle strength.

The following pages contain a sample twelve week bounding program. **NOTICE:** Week number six is a maintenance level. By adhering to the week six program, you can maintain the strength and power achieved after the completion of the twelfth week.

POWER BOUNDS

	Monday	Tuesday	Wednesday	Thursday	Friday
Week 1	3 x 20	3 x 20	3 x 20	3 x 20	3 x 20
Week 2	3 x 25	3 x 25	3 x 25	3 x 25	3 x 25
Week 3	3 x 30	3 x 30	3 x 30	3 x 30	3 x 30
Week 4	3 x 35	3 x 35	3 x 35	3 x 35	3 x 35
Week 5	3 x 35	3 x 35	3 x 35	3 x 35	3 x 35
Week 6	3 x 35	3 x 35	3 x 35	3 x 35	3 x 35
Week 7	3 x 35	3 x 35	3 x 35	3 x 35	3 x 35
Week 8	3 x 35	3 x 35	3 x 35	3 x 35	3 x 35
Week 9	3 x 35	3 x 35	3 x 35	3 x 35	3 x 35
Week 10	3 x 35	3 x 35	3 x 35	3 x 35	3 x 35
Week 11	3 x 35	3 x 35	3 x 35	3 x 35	3 x 35
Week 12	3 x 35	3 x 35	3 x 35	3 x 35	3 x 35

STEP-UPS

	Monday	Tuesday	Wednesday	Thursday	Friday
Week 1	1 x 100	1 x 100	1 x 100	1 x 100	1 x 100
Week 2	1 x 110	1 x 110	1 x 110	1 x 110	1 x 110
Week 3	1 x 120	1 x 120	1 x 120	1 x 120	1 x 120
Week 4	1 x 130	1 x 130	1 x 130	1 x 130	1 x 130
Week 5	1 x 140	1 x 140	1 x 140	1 x 140	1 x 140
Week 6	1 x 150	1 x 150	1 x 150	1 x 150	1 x 150
Week 7	1 x 160	1 x 160	1 x 160	1 x 160	1 x 160
Week 8	1 x 170	1 x 170	1 x 170	1 x 170	1 x 170
Week 9	1 x 180	1 x 180	1 x 180	1 x 180	1 x 180
Week 10	1 x 190	1 x 190	1 x 190	1 x 190	1 x 190
Week 11	1 x 200	1 x 200	1 x 200	1 x 200	1 x 200
Week 12	1 x 200	1 x 200	1 x 200	1 x 200	1 x 200

KNEE BENDS

	Monday	Tuesday	Wednesday	Thursday	Friday
Week 1	1 x 100	1 x 100	1 x 100	1 x 100	1 x 100
Week 2	1 x 110	1 x 110	1 x 110	1 x 110	1 x 110
Week 3	1 x 120	1 x 120	1 x 120	1 x 120	1 x 120
Week 4	1 x 130	1 x 130	1 x 130	1 x 130	1 x 130
Week 5	1 x 140	1 x 140	1 x 140	1 x 140	1 x 140
Week 6	1 x 150	1 x 150	1 x 150	1 x 150	1 x 150
Week 7	1 x 150	1 x 150	1 x 150	1 x 150	1 x 150
Week 8	1 x 150	1 x 150	1 x 150	1 x 150	1 x 150
Week 9	1 x 150	1 x 150	1 x 150	1 x 150	1 x 150
Week 10	1 x 150	1 x 150	1 x 150	1 x 150	1 x 150
Week 11	1 x 150	1 x 150	1 x 150	1 x 150	1 x 150
Week 12	1 x 150	1 x 150	1 x 150	1 x 150	1 x 150

CALF RAISES

	Monday	Tuesday	Wednesday	Thursday	Friday
Week 1	1 x 30	1 x 30	1 x 30	1 x 30	1 x 30
Week 2	1 x 30	1 x 30	1 x 30	1 x 30	1 x 30
Week 3	1 x 40	1 x 40	1 x 40	1 x 40	1 x 40
Week 4	1 x 40	1 x 40	1 x 40	1 x 40	1 x 40
Week 5	1 x 50	1 x 50	1 x 50	1 x 50	1 x 50
Week 6	1 x 50	1 x 50	1 x 50	1 x 50	1 x 50
Week 7	1 x 60	1 x 60	1 x 60	1 x 60	1 x 60
Week 8	1 x 60	1 x 60	1 x 60	1 x 60	1 x 60
Week 9	1 x 60	1 x 60	1 x 60	1 x 60	1 x 60
Week 10	1 x 60	1 x 60	1 x 60	1 x 60	1 x 60
Week 11	1 x 60	1 x 60	1 x 60	1 x 60	1 x 60
Week 12	1 x 60	1 x 60	1 x 60	1 x 60	1 x 60

Recommended Reading

Anderson, Bob. *Stretching*. Shelter Publications, Bolinas, California, 1980.

Avella, Douglas G., and DiGeronimo, Theresa Foy. *Raising a Healthy Athlete*. British American Publishing, Latham, New York, 1990.

Bast, Carol J., and Wolterstorff, Amy. *Masters Guide to Sport Camps* (South Edition, West Edition, Midwest Edition, and National Edition). Masters Press. Grand Rapids, Michigan. The latest edition can be ordered by writing to:
>Masters Press
>124 East Fulton Street, Suite 600
>Grand Rapids, Michigan 49503
>or by phone at 1-800-72-CAMPS

Callahan, Timothy. *Callahan's College Guide to Athletics and Academics in America*. Harper & Row Publisher, New York, 1984.

Green, Alan. *The Directory of Athletic Scholarships*. Tilden Press, New York, New York, 1987.

Green, Gordon. *Getting Straight A's*. Carol Publishing Group, New York, 1993.

Jensen, Eric. *Student Success Secrets*. Barron's Educational Series, Inc., Hauppauge, New York, 1989.

Mauro, Bob. *College Athletic Scholarships*. New York: McFarland & Co., 1988.

Peterson's Guides, Inc. *Peterson's Sports Scholarships and College Athletic Programs*. Peterson's Guides, Inc., Princeton, New Jersey, 1994.

Reynolds, Bill. *Weight Training for Beginners*. Contemporary Books, Chicago, Illinois, 1982.

Schreiber, Lee R. *The Parents' Guide to Kids' Sports*. Little, Brown, and Company, Boston, MA 1990.

Sprague, Ken . *Sports Strength*. Perigee Books, published by The Putnam Publishing Group, New York, New York, 1993.

Time Life Books. *Restoring the Body*. Alexandria, Virginia: Time—Life Inc., 1987.

Bibliography

Chany, Kalman A. *The Student Access Guide to Paying for College*. New York: Villard Books, 1992.

Colgan, Michael, M.D. *Optimum Sports Nutrition*. Advanced Research Press, Ronkonkoma, New York, 1993.

Haas, Robert, M.D. *Eat To Win*. New American Library, New York, New York.

Hopper, Chris. *The Sports-Confident Child*. Pantheon Books, New York, 1988.

Kilbler, W. Ben, M.D. *The Sport Preparticipation Fitness Examination*. Human Kinetics Books, Champaign, Illinois, 1990.

Lindsey, Ruth; Jones, Billie; Whitley, Ada Van. *Fitness*. William C. Brown Co. Publishers, Dubuque, Iowa, 1983.

National Collegiate Athletic Association. "NCAA academic, graduation research is published." NCAA NEWS, 1991.

Southmayd, William, M.D. and Hoffman, Marshall. *Sports Health*. Perigee Books, published by The Putnam Publishing Group, New York, New York. 1981.

Spink, Kevin S. *Give Your Kids a Sporting Chance*. Toronto: Summerhill Press, 1988.

Wolff, Rick, *Good Sports*. New York: Dell Publishing, 1993.

Index

NOTES

NOTES

NOTES

NOTES

MORE NEWS AT YOUR FINGERTIPS...

IF YOU PURCHASED How To Get An Athletic Scholarship you are entitled to a free subscription (4 issues) to Student-Athletes News (a $12.00 value). To order, send the original sales receipt and self-addressed stamped envelope to the publisher (see copyright page for address), and request a subscription to Student-Athlete News.

IF YOU BORROWED THIS BOOK you are entitled to a free subscription to SAN, however you must purchase a copy of the book and order as directed above. Contact the publisher to find a book seller near you or to order a paid subscription to SAN.

STUDENT-ATHLETE NEWS FEATURES:

Profiles of colleges/camps/collegiate athletes
The latest and best training routines
Program rankings, by sport, covering the national associations
"New product" reports
Interviews with college and pro athletes
Careers in athletics
Rule updates and changes
Financial Aid
High performance diets/recipes
College surveys
Reports on the major associations
Multi-sport training techniques

Special "HOW-TO" features, step-by-step:
Create a well written resume
Create a video resume
Develop a student-athlete
Put together a "recruitment kit"

DATE			